282.—BROAD BEAN.

VICIA FABA.   M. (1565) 420.

wers purple, or white with a black spot on the wings.   3 ft.   Fields and gardens.   June—July.

es are shown with too many flowers, which should be from 2 to 4.   They were probably drawn
ry, when the plant was in fruit.   The plant is here altogether too stunted.   The execution of the
ery admirable, and the figure gives an excellent suggestion for modelling.

Moosewood Restaurant Simple Suppers

Moosewood Restaurant
Simple Suppers

Fresh Ideas for the Weeknight Table

The Moosewood Collective

Photography: Jim Scherer
Food Stylist: Catrine Kelty

Clarkson Potter/Publishers

New York

We dedicate this book to all who work for peace

Published in the United States by Clarkson Potter/Publishers, New York, an imprint
of the Crown Publishing Group, a division of Random House, Inc.
www.crownpublishing.com
www.clarksonpotter.com

CLARKSON N. POTTER is a trademark and POTTER and colophon are registered
trademarks of Random House, Inc.

Library of Congress Cataloging-in-Publication Data
Moosewood restaurant simple suppers: fresh ideas for the weeknight
table / the Moosewood Collective.
    p.   cm.
1. Suppers.   2. Quick and easy cookery.   3. Moosewood Restaurant.
I. Moosewood Collective.
TX738.M66   2005
641.5'55—dc22   2004022024

ISBN: 0-609-60912-2

Printed in Japan

Design by Memo Productions, NY

10   9   8   7   6   5   4   3

acknowledgments

As Moosewood cooks and cookbook authors, we share a common experience: Our friends and families are afraid to cook for us. They think we expect a gourmet meal when honestly, after a long day of chopping mountains of vegetables, we are grateful for the simplest fare. So thanks to all of you who set aside your worries and nurtured us with good food and companionship. We hope this collection of recipes will inspire you to invite us over more often!

We wish to thank our Moosewood Restaurant partners for running the show while we were testing recipes and writing this book: Joan Adler, Ned Asta, Tony Del Plato, David Dietrich, Neil Minnis, Eliana Parra, Sara Robbins, and Myoko Maureen Vivino. We also wish to express appreciation to our hardworking employees.

Our affection and thanks go out to our friends and agents, Arnold and Elise Goodman. We greatly appreciate the careful eye and expert guidance of our editors at Clarkson Potter, Pam Krauss, Jennifer DeFilippi, and Rica Allannic. We also send special thanks to Marysarah Quinn for her admirable work as the creative director on this book. Her calm, competent influence has been invaluable to us. Thanks again to our designers Jan Derevjanik and Laura Palese for doing a beautiful job. And thanks also to the rest of the Clarkson Potter staff for their enthusiastic, friendly help.

We wish to express our appreciation to our photographer, Jim Scherer, and food stylist, Catrine Kelty, for creating graceful photographs for our book. We admire your artistry and dedication to your craft.

And finally, without the technical expertise and the good-natured patience of Emilio Del Plato, we would have been a sorry, frustrated bunch who did not see our computers as our friends during the process of preparing the manuscript. Thank you, Emilio.

contents

Fettuccine with Fresh Herbs (page 24)

introduction

When we cook at Moosewood Restaurant, we often make complex dishes with lots of ingredi-ents, building layer upon layer of flavor. Fresh vegetables, herbs, and fruits are delivered to our kitchen daily. We have good equipment, and our spice rack is extensive. There are two or three or four (sometimes more) of us in the kitchen at the same time. Prep cooks make some of the component parts of dishes ahead of time, and we have bussers and dishwashers to clean up our mess. But often we're still pushing to get the work done by "show time."

At home, we want to relieve the pressure. We crave simple food. We don't want cooking at home to be the breakneck performance it is in the restaurant but rather a small pleasure, relaxed enough that we can enjoy the process as well as the results. We're not alone in finding this idea appealing. When we mentioned to friends that we were thinking of doing a book of recipes for simple suppers, inevitably they exclaimed, "That's the one I need" or "Write that book for me." And so we have.

Everyone needs a few dishes that they like to make over and over, recipes that can be messed with a bit for tasty, comforting, and hassle-free meals. When you ask people what their favorite dish is, most don't name some-thing elaborate that they can only get at a particular

Tomato Tortilla Soup (page 117),
Bean & Cheese Quesadillas (page 141)

restaurant. Usually the favorite is something simple they've had a hundred times at home, something reliable—always good, every time.

When our ideas for this cookbook started percolating, we discussed the meaning of *simple* a lot. To some it meant a minimal number of ingredients in each recipe, and to others it was a matter of time: 30 minutes or less to get the meal on the table, or not having to make an extra trip to the grocery store. One of us wanted to count the number of pots in the sink at the end of the meal. As our individual ideas began to cross-pollinate, we decided that recipes would qualify for this book in several ways. These recipes have fewer ingredients than our usual, and we've made good use of trustworthy convenience products (vegetable broths, salsas, slaw mixes) and nonperishable pantry items (spices, canned beans, condiments). Some of the simplest recipes depend on high-quality fresh ingredients, and with good produce, you don't have to do much to make a delectable meal.

Not all everyday cooking has to be a race with the clock, but a lot of our recipes are either quick to make or the hands-on time is short, and then you need to do very little or nothing while the dish stews or bakes. (Love those one-pot meals. Fewer pots, easier cleanup.) Some dishes can be prepared ahead of time and then served with very little fuss. A few are designed to be assembled at the table by diners.

Here you'll find simple recipes that are tried-and-true. And when we have something extra to say, we've added ingredient and cooking notes (substitutions or variations, hints about different cooking techniques, tips for cooking ahead, suggestions for leftovers). We try to keep it real about what constitutes a meal, also. You might want to serve bread with a stew or a green salad with pasta, but each of our main-dish recipes can stand alone as a satisfying simple supper. That said, we include serving and menu ideas for when you want to do more or would like to combine dishes for variety. Sometimes a side dish can become a main dish with a little modification. And because everyone needs something sweet now and then, we suggest desserts that we think complement the main dish.

To help make supper simpler, first and foremost we recommend a well-stocked pantry. We've made a list of what we find useful to keep on hand in the cupboard, refrigerator, and freezer. In the Guide to Ingredients, Tools & Techniques, we include shopping tips and basic information about ingredients and cooking techniques, and recommend a few kitchen tools.

When we write a cookbook, we test and retest the recipes, trying lots of possibilities. We draw on ideas from everywhere, and then we improvise and adapt. We focus on details and endlessly discuss the fine points with each other, working to get it just right so that we'll have recipes that really work. Of course, supper doesn't have to be perfect to be wonderful. We hope that when you're at home making something to eat, you'll relax. If you don't have the pasta shape we recommend, use a different one. If you forgot to restock the nutmeg, oh well— do without. If you don't have time to make rice, have couscous. Let the seasonal availability of fresh fruits and vegetables be your inspiration as much as any recipe.

The idea of simple suppers strikes a chord within us all. Despite being busier than ever in an increasingly complicated world, people still want to eat well. And even though we want you to come to our restaurant and let us cook for you, we also think it's important to cook and eat at home. Cooking something good can make you feel good—and then eating something good and feeding the people you love can make you feel even better. We hope this cookbook will help make suppertime a welcome, peaceful time of your day.

Pasta with Olives Piquant (page 19)

pasta

selecting & cooking pasta

Often, pasta is what we think of first when we want to make a quick, simple supper. It provides a great canvas for improvisation, and fresh, tasty sauces and toppings can be made in the same time it takes to boil water and cook the pasta itself. Many pasta dishes are complete meals in themselves; others need little more than a green salad to round out the meal.

There is a multitude of shapes and sizes of pasta, and there is a certain logic in pairing sauces and toppings with particular shapes. In general, long strands such as spaghetti and linguine work well with tomato sauces and pestos. Bowl-shaped cuts such as orecchiette and shells are good to serve with chunky vegetable sauces because the pasta catches and holds the vegetable pieces. Flat noodles like fettuccine and farfalle go well with delicate cream and cheese sauces. That said, we would never let the lack of the perfect pasta shape stop us from going ahead with the sauce we want to make. In our recipes, we specify a particular pasta when we think it matters; otherwise, we leave it up to you. In the Guide to Ingredients, Tools & Techniques, you'll find brief descriptions of some pasta shapes (see page 291).

The pasta lovers among Moosewood cooks stock their home pantries with a variety of imported Italian pastas. Here's why made in Italy matters: Pasta has been produced commercially in Italy since 1400, and still today, most of the best pastas are made there because the Italian government enforces strict national standards for ingredients and manufacturing processes, which results in a high-quality product, superior to most of our domestic pastas. Old ways are the best ways with pasta making, it seems. For instance, when pasta is extruded through bronze rather than Teflon dies, it has a rougher, more porous texture. When pasta is dried slowly at low temperatures, the protein is not denatured and the pasta is firmer when cooked. We recommend DeCecco, Barilla, and Bionaturae brands.

Cook pasta following these basic guidelines: Serve about one-fourth pound of pasta per person. Cook pasta in a large pot with plenty of water so that it quickly returns to a boil after the pasta is added and so that the pasta has room to float freely, which helps it cook evenly. Use about 4 or 5 quarts of salted water per pound of pasta. Ease the pasta into rapidly boiling water, stir to separate, and cover the pot. When the water returns to a boil, remove the lid and stir again.

Fresh pasta cooks in just a minute or two. The time needed to cook dried pasta depends on its thickness; don't trust the time suggested on the pasta box—it's sometimes too long. The only way to know when pasta is ready is to taste it. Several minutes before you expect the pasta to be done, start testing it every minute so you'll catch it when it is al dente—that is, tender but with a firm bite. Drain it in a colander and transfer to a serving bowl.

Pasta is best eaten while it is hot, so it's nice to heat the serving bowl. The simplest way to do that is to place a colander in your serving bowl in the sink. When the pasta is done, pour it into the colander, lift the colander, and leave the hot water in the bowl for a minute. Then just pour the water down the drain and transfer the pasta to the now warm bowl. The bowl can also be warmed in a 200° oven while the pasta cooks.

creamy lemon pasta ⌒

In Comfort Me with Apples, *Ruth Reichl attributes the original recipe to Danny Kaye, but lemon and cream seems such a simple, natural combination that we suppose people were putting it on pasta long before Danny Kaye was born.*

SERVES 4

TIME: 15 MINUTES

1 lemon
¼ cup unsalted butter
1 cup heavy cream
1 pound fresh fettuccine or dried spaghettini
1 cup grated Parmesan cheese
salt and pepper

Bring a large covered pot of salted water to a boil. Meanwhile, grate the lemon peel (about 2 teaspoons of zest, see page 295) and squeeze the lemon (about 3 tablespoons of juice).

In a small skillet or saucepan on low heat, melt the butter. Stir in the cream and heat gently. Stir in the lemon juice and zest. Turn off the heat.

When the water boils, cook the pasta until al dente (2 or 3 minutes for fresh pasta, longer for dried). Set aside a cup of the hot pasta-cooking water and drain the pasta.

Place the hot drained pasta in a large serving bowl, add the lemon cream sauce, and toss. Add some or all of the reserved hot water if more liquid is needed. Toss in the grated Parmesan. Season to taste with salt and pepper.

variations ⌒

Add 2 tablespoons of finely chopped chives, about a cup of hot, cooked green peas, and some red pepper flakes when you add the cheese.

For a lighter version, use olive oil in place of butter and half-and-half instead of cream. If you have some arugula in your refrigerator, here's a great way to use it up: Put about 3 cups of loosely packed arugula leaves in the bottom of the serving bowl; it will wilt when you add the hot pasta.

pasta with olives piquant ∾

*So easy to make, yet simply delectable—if you keep an assort-
ment of good deli olives on hand, supper is only minutes
away. (See photo on page 14.)*

SERVES 4 TO 6

TIME: 25 MINUTES

1 pound spaghetti or other pasta
1½ cups assorted pitted olives
4 garlic cloves, minced
3 tablespoons olive oil
½ cup minced fresh parsley
¼ teaspoon crushed red pepper flakes (optional)
grated Pecorino Romano or Parmesan cheese (optional)

Bring a large covered pot of salted water to a boil. Add the pasta and cook until al dente.

Meanwhile, mince the olives by hand or in a food processor. If you use a food processor, pulse the olives for only a few seconds—until finely chopped but not pasty.

In a heavy skillet on low heat, cook the garlic in the oil until golden. Add the parsley, red pepper flakes, and chopped olives. Cook, stirring constantly, just until the parsley is wilted and the olives are heated through. Remove from the heat.

When the pasta is done, reserve a cup of the cooking water, then drain the pasta and place it in a serving bowl. Add the olive mixture (swirl some of the cooking water in the skillet to get the last bits of olive out). Toss, and if the pasta needs more moisture, add more of the cooking water. Serve topped with grated cheese if you wish.

INGREDIENT NOTE Choose a selection of olives, being sure to include kalamatas for their rich, briny taste, and some meaty big green olives. Olives stuffed with pimientos, garlic, or lemon peel will add bits of color and flavor.

serving & menu ideas ∾

Pasta with Olives Piquant served with Lemony Green Beans (page 192) makes a great meal, and it's easy to prepare both in about 30 minutes. Or try Fresh Tomato & Mozzarella Salad (page 213), served alongside or tossed with the pasta.

pasta with tomatoes,
summer & winter ↀ

*Pasta with tomatoes may be the most fundamental and satisfying
simple supper—it's fast, versatile, and always good, time after
time. In the winter, spaghetti and tomato sauce with cheese hits
the spot. In the summer, we never tire of pasta with good
ripe tomatoes, fresh mozzarella, and fresh basil.*

SERVES 4

TIME: 25 MINUTES

1 pound pasta
Simple Tomato Sauce (page 251) or Fresh Tomato & Mozzarella
  Salad (page 213)
grated Pecorino Romano or Parmesan cheese (optional)

Bring a large covered pot of salted water to a boil. Add the pasta and cook until al dente.

Meanwhile, prepare Simple Tomato Sauce or Fresh Tomato & Mozzarella Salad.

When the pasta is done, drain it and top with sauce and grated cheese, or toss with the tomatoes and mozzarella.

INGREDIENT NOTE Any shape of pasta is fine, but a short, chunky pasta (see page 291) goes best with Fresh Tomato & Mozzarella Salad, and tomato sauce is traditionally paired with long strands.

serving & menu ideas ↀ

A green salad is a tried-and-true accompaniment. Another tasty side dish is Lemony Green Beans (page 192). Have Sweet Spiced Nuts (page 261) and a glass of port for dessert.

pasta with greens & ricotta ～

Mustard greens and broccoli raab (also called brocoletti di rape, rape, and rapini) are somewhat bitter, a good counterpoint to creamy, subtly flavored ricotta cheese.

SERVES 4 TO 6

TIME: 25 MINUTES

1 bunch mustard greens or broccoli raab (about 1 pound)

1 pound penne, fusilli, or other short chunky pasta

6 garlic cloves, minced or pressed

1 tablespoon olive oil

1 teaspoon salt

¼ teaspoon black pepper

15 ounces ricotta cheese

1 cup grated Pecorino Romano or Parmesan cheese

Bring a large covered pot of salted water to a boil. Meanwhile, remove the tough stems from the mustard greens and chop the leaves. If using broccoli raab, discard the bottom ½ inch of the stems and chop the rest. Rinse and drain the greens.

When the water boils, cook the pasta until al dente.

While the pasta cooks, in a large skillet or pot on low heat, cook the garlic in the oil until golden. Add a couple of handfuls of the still damp greens to the skillet and stir until wilted. Continue adding greens and stirring until all of the greens are in the skillet. Add some of the pasta-cooking water, if needed, to prevent sticking, and cook until the greens are tender but still bright green. Add the salt and pepper and remove from the heat.

In a large serving bowl, stir about ½ cup of pasta cooking water into the ricotta cheese and whisk until smooth. When the pasta is done, drain it, and add to the ricotta. Add the wilted greens and ½ cup of the grated cheese and toss well. Add more salt and pepper to taste. Serve topped with the rest of the grated cheese.

serving & menu ideas ～

Beet Salad (page 209) or Carrot Salad with Raspberry Vinaigrette (page 217) looks beautiful and tastes great with this pasta.

pasta with broccoli, edamame & walnuts ∿

Shelled edamame (fresh soybeans) are available in the frozen food section of many natural foods stores and supermarkets. Whole wheat pasta is especially good in this dish. If you think you'll be lucky enough to have leftovers for lunch tomorrow, instead of tossing the walnuts into the pasta, sprinkle them on top of each serving.

SERVES 4 TO 6

TIME: 20 MINUTES

¾ pound chunky pasta

¼ cup olive oil

4 garlic cloves, minced or pressed

3 cups bite-sized pieces of broccoli

1 cup frozen shelled edamame

¾ teaspoon salt

¼ cup chopped fresh basil, oregano, thyme, or marjoram

1 cup chopped toasted walnuts

salt and pepper

grated Parmesan or Pecorino Romano cheese (optional)

Bring a large covered pot of salted water to a boil. Add the pasta and cook until al dente.

Meanwhile, warm 2 tablespoons of the olive oil in a large skillet on low heat. Add the garlic and cook for a few seconds. Add the broccoli with about ½ cup of the hot pasta-cooking water, turn the heat to high, and cook for about 2 minutes. Add the edamame, salt, and herbs. Continue to cook until the water evaporates and the broccoli is crisp-tender and bright green, about 5 minutes. Remove from the heat.

When the pasta is done, drain it. In a serving bowl, toss the pasta with the vegetable mixture, the remaining 2 tablespoons of olive oil, and the toasted chopped walnuts. Season with salt and pepper. Serve topped with grated cheese if you wish.

INGREDIENT NOTE In place of fresh herbs, add about 2 teaspoons of dried herbs to the skillet with the broccoli.

serving & menu ideas ∾

Have some Butterscotch Icebox Cookies (page 279) or a 5-Minute Milkshake (page 281) for dessert.

fettuccine with fresh herbs ↬

Fresh summer herbs release an intense, splendid aroma when you stir them into hot oil. (See photo on page 10.)

SERVES 4 TO 6

TIME: 20 MINUTES

1 pound fettuccine or other pasta
¼ cup extra-virgin olive oil
4 garlic cloves, minced or pressed
½ cup minced fresh parsley
½ cup minced fresh basil
½ cup minced chives or scallions
½ teaspoon salt
½ teaspoon black pepper
grated Parmesan or Pecorino Romano cheese (optional)

Bring a large covered pot of salted water to a boil. Add the pasta and cook until al dente.

Meanwhile, prepare the garlic and herbs. Warm the oil in a small pan on low heat. Add the garlic and cook for about a minute until the garlic is golden; don't let it brown. Add the herbs and cook for about 30 seconds, stirring constantly. Remove from the heat, ladle about ½ cup of the hot pasta-cooking water into the pan, and set aside.

When the pasta is done, drain it. Place the drained pasta in a serving bowl, add the herb and oil mixture and the salt and pepper, and toss well. Toss in some grated cheese if you like. Serve right away.

INGREDIENT NOTE If you have a garden filled with herbs, you may want to add some other fresh herbs such as thyme, sage, marjoram, mint, chervil, oregano, or summer savory.

serving & menu ideas ↬

Serve with one of the Crostini (page 136) as a first course, or with Fresh Tomato & Mozzarella Salad (page 213) on the side.

fettuccine with walnut pesto ‿

Rich and delicious Walnut Pesto can be made in minutes in a food processor or blender—it will be ready before the pasta has cooked. Make extra; it keeps well for 3 or 4 days in the refrigerator and is good on boiled potatoes and steamed fish.

SERVES 4 TO 6

TIME: 20 MINUTES

1 pound fettuccine or other pasta

WALNUT PESTO

1 cup chopped fresh or canned tomatoes
2 garlic cloves, minced or pressed
1 tablespoon extra-virgin olive oil
$\frac{1}{2}$ teaspoon salt
1 cup toasted walnuts

$\frac{1}{2}$ cup very thinly sliced fresh basil leaves (optional)
1 cup grated Pecorino Romano or Parmesan cheese (optional)

Bring a large covered pot of salted water to a boil. Add the pasta and cook until al dente. Reserve about a cup of the pasta-cooking liquid and then drain.

Meanwhile, make the Walnut Pesto: In a blender or food processor, purée the tomatoes, garlic, olive oil, and salt for a few seconds, until smooth. Add the walnuts and process until an even-colored and somewhat lumpy paste is formed. If you're using fresh tomatoes, you might need to add 1 or 2 tablespoons of water to the mixture.

Transfer the drained pasta to a serving bowl. Toss the pasta with the Walnut Pesto, adding enough reserved cooking liquid to make it saucy. Serve immediately, topped with basil and grated cheese, if you wish.

serving & menu ideas ‿

Serve with a simple green vegetable, such as broccoli or sautéed greens, or with a spinach salad with Caesar Dressing (page 220). Make Watercress Crostini (page 136) to munch on until the pasta is ready.

pasta with caramelized onions & blue cheese ∾

Here's a simple supper to make in the chill of fall or winter, when the sweetness of the onions and the richness of the cheese is comforting.

SERVES 4 TO 6

TIME: 30 MINUTES

1 pound chunky pasta

1 tablespoon olive oil

6 cups chopped onions

1 teaspoon salt

¼ teaspoon black pepper

½ cup dry white wine, vegetable broth, or water

4 ounces crumbled blue cheese (1 cup)

Bring a large covered pot of salted water to a boil. Add the pasta and cook until al dente.

Meanwhile, in a skillet on medium heat, warm the oil and cook the onions with the salt and pepper until soft, golden brown, and lightly caramelized. (The larger your skillet, the faster the onions will caramelize. In a 12- or 14-inch skillet, the process may take less than 10 minutes. In a smaller skillet in which the onions are crowded, it could take 20 minutes.) Add the wine, broth, or water and continue to cook on low heat, stirring occasionally, until the pasta is done. If the onions begin to stick, add some pasta-cooking water.

When the pasta is done, drain it, reserving a cup of the hot water. Place the pasta in a serving bowl, add the onions (swirl some of the reserved water around in the skillet to get out every tasty bit) and the blue cheese, and toss together to melt the cheese and coat the pasta. Add more of the pasta-cooking water if you'd like it saucier. Serve hot.

serving & menu ideas ∾

A salad with slightly bitter greens goes well with this sweet, rich pasta. Or toss endive with Toasted Pecan Vinaigrette (page 222). Peach Brown Betty (page 268) is a sweet ending.

spaghetti with sun-dried tomatoes & pine nuts ∿

This traditional southern Italian pasta recipe, with its base of aglio e olio, garlic and oil, is one of those rustic foods that presents like a gourmet dish. It's made entirely with pantry items, so it's a perfect last-minute supper.

SERVES 4 TO 6

TIME: 25 MINUTES

½ cup sun-dried tomatoes
1 pound spaghetti
3 tablespoons extra-virgin olive oil
8 to 10 garlic cloves, minced or pressed
¼ cup toasted pine nuts
¼ cup minced fresh parsley (optional)
salt and pepper to taste
grated Parmesan or crumbled ricotta salata (optional)

Place the sun-dried tomatoes in a heatproof bowl, cover with boiling water, and set aside to soften for about 15 minutes. Meanwhile, bring a large covered pot of salted water to a boil. Add the pasta and cook until al dente.

While the pasta cooks, in a small pan on low heat or in a microwave-safe bowl, heat the oil and garlic until golden. Set aside. Drain the sun-dried tomatoes, reserving the soaking liquid. Cut the tomatoes into thin strips.

When the pasta is done, drain it and place in a serving bowl. Add the cooked garlic, sun-dried tomato strips, pine nuts, and parsley. Toss well. Stir in some of the reserved sun-dried tomato soaking liquid to moisten the pasta, if needed. Season with salt and pepper. Serve hot, topped with grated cheese if you like.

INGREDIENT NOTES Add chopped fresh tomatoes, a couple tablespoons of capers or sliced olives, and/or some thinly sliced fresh fennel (sauté it in the oil before adding the garlic).

serving & menu ideas ∿

Have a tossed green salad and enjoy Mocha Sorbet (page 272) for dessert.

pasta with artichoke hearts & feta ❧

Feta cheese, garlic, and artichoke hearts are some of our favorite ingredients; here, they're combined in a very simple pasta dish that packs a lot of flavor. For this dish, we make an instant creamy sauce by stirring hot pasta-cooking water into feta.

SERVES 4 TO 6

TIME: 30 MINUTES

1 pound pasta

2 cups chopped onions

3 garlic cloves, minced or pressed

2 teaspoons dried oregano

3 tablespoons extra-virgin olive oil

2 14-ounce cans of artichoke hearts, drained and quartered

¼ cup chopped fresh parsley

1½ cups crumbled feta cheese

Bring a large covered pot of salted water to a boil. Add the pasta and cook until al dente.

Meanwhile, in a skillet on medium-high heat, cook the onions, garlic, and oregano in the oil, stirring frequently, until the onions soften and are turning brown at the edges, about 7 minutes. Add the artichoke hearts and cook until heated through, a couple of minutes. Remove from the heat and stir in the parsley.

When the pasta is done, drain it, reserving 1½ cups of the pasta-cooking liquid. In a serving bowl, whisk the reserved liquid into the feta until smooth. Add the pasta and the artichoke mixture and toss.

INGREDIENT NOTE Spinach fettuccine or linguine looks and tastes good in this dish, but any pasta is fine.

serving & menu ideas ❧

Add color and sweetness to the meal with Marmalade-Glazed Carrots (page 196) on the side and Mocha Sorbet (page 272) for dessert.

beijing noodles ∾

Here's a meatless variation of a classic northern Chinese noodle dish. We love the contrast between the hot, saucy noodles and the cold, crunchy raw vegetable toppings. The sauce will keep in the refrigerator for 3 or 4 days, so you can make the sauce and prepare the toppings ahead of time and then cook the noodles when you're ready to eat.

SERVES 4 TO 6

TIME: 45 MINUTES

$\frac{1}{2}$ ounce dried shiitake mushrooms (5 to 8 caps)

$1\frac{1}{2}$ cups boiling water

1 cake firm tofu (about 16 ounces)

12 ounces moonlight mushrooms

2 large garlic cloves

1 large onion

1 tablespoon vegetable oil

$\frac{1}{2}$ teaspoon salt

$\frac{1}{8}$ teaspoon black pepper

$\frac{3}{4}$ cup Chinese sweet bean sauce (6-ounce can)

3 tablespoons white or cider vinegar

1 pound linguine or Chinese wheat noodles

1 CUP EACH OF AT LEAST THREE OF THE FOLLOWING TOPPINGS:

∾ grated carrots

∾ chopped tomatoes

∾ mung bean sprouts

∾ shredded cabbage

∾ peeled, seeded, and diced cucumbers

∾ a few sliced scallions

Place the dried shiitake in a bowl, add the boiling water, and set aside to soften for about 15 minutes. With a box grater or in a food processor, coarsely grate the tofu. Slice the

(recipe continued on next page)

moonlight mushrooms, mince or press the garlic, and chop the onion. Bring a large covered pot of salted water to a boil for cooking the pasta.

In a large skillet on medium heat, warm the oil and sauté the onion, garlic, salt, and pepper for about 7 minutes, until the onions are translucent. Stir in the sliced mushrooms and grated tofu and cook, stirring frequently, for about 5 minutes, until the mushrooms begin to release their juices.

Meanwhile, remove the softened shiitake from the bowl. If there are large stems, cut them off and discard. Slice the caps and add to the skillet. Add ¾ cup of the shiitake soaking liquid (pour the liquid with care so that any gritty residue is left behind in the bowl). Add the sweet bean sauce and the vinegar and stir occasionally until the sauce is hot, about 5 minutes. If the sauce is too thick, add a little water.

While the sauce is simmering, cook the pasta until al dente and prepare the toppings; we like to serve the toppings at the table in separate bowls so that diners can choose their own. Drain the pasta.

Serve Beijing Noodles in individual bowls: a helping of noodles topped with some sauce, and then the toppings.

INGREDIENT NOTES Look for Chinese sweet bean sauce in Asian markets. It usually comes in 6- or 16-ounce cans. Leftover sauce can be stored in a jar in the refrigerator for several months.
  Stir some Chinese chili paste into the sauce.
  Stir a few drops of dark sesame oil into the noodles.

serving & menu idea ∾
....
If you want a simple dessert, try the Orange Vanilla Shake (page 281).

whole-grain pasta with greens & tomatoes ∾

Whole wheat and spelt pastas have a pleasant, nutty flavor that stands up to the flavors in this sauce, but any kind of pasta is fine for this recipe.

SERVES 4

TIME: 30 MINUTES

12 ounces whole wheat or spelt pasta

1 medium head of curly endive or escarole (about 12 ounces)

5 garlic cloves, pressed or minced

2 tablespoons olive oil

¼ teaspoon salt

1 28-ounce can of diced tomatoes

¼ teaspoon dried oregano

¼ teaspoon crumbled dried rosemary (½ teaspoon minced fresh)

grated Parmesan cheese (optional)

chopped olives (optional)

Bring a large pot of salted water to a boil for cooking the pasta. Meanwhile, rinse and chop the endive or escarole and set aside to drain.

When the water boils, add the pasta and cook until until al dente. While the pasta cooks, in a large skillet or saucepan on medium-high heat, cook the garlic in the oil until it sizzles. Add the greens, sprinkle with the salt, and cook until wilted, stirring often. Stir in the tomatoes, oregano, and rosemary. Cover and simmer on low heat, stirring occasionally, until the pasta is done.

When the pasta is done, drain it and toss with a little olive oil if you wish. Serve the pasta topped with the sauce and some grated cheese and/or chopped olives.

serving & menu ideas ∾

After such a wholesome supper, treat yourself to Riesling Roasted Pears (page 264) or Orange-Almond Polenta Cake (page 266).

Tofu Hijiki Sauté (page 52)

sautés, curries & more

jop chai ∿

Here's a Moosewood version of one of our favorite meals in Korean restaurants—easy enough to make at home.

SERVES 4

TIME: 40 MINUTES

4 ounces bean thread noodles

1 tablespoon vegetable oil

$1\frac{1}{2}$ cups thinly sliced onions

3 garlic cloves, minced

3 cups thinly sliced green cabbage or coleslaw mix

1 cup thinly sliced red bell peppers

8 ounces veggie crumbles

SAUCE

$\frac{1}{4}$ cup soy sauce

3 tablespoons rice vinegar or cider vinegar

$\frac{1}{2}$ cup water

1 teaspoon dark sesame oil

Soak the bean thread noodles in hot tap water to cover until softened, about 15 to 20 minutes. When soft, drain and cut into more easily eaten lengths, 4 to 5 inches (kitchen scissors are handy for this task). To keep the noodles from clumping, toss them with a little dark sesame oil or vegetable oil.

While the noodles are soaking, heat the oil in a large pan or wok, add the onions and garlic, and sauté for about 2 minutes. Add the cabbage and sauté for a couple of minutes. Stir in the peppers and continue to sauté until the vegetables are crisp-tender. Add the veggie crumbles and cook for another minute or two. Combine the sauce ingredients and add them to the vegetables. Add the drained noodles and cook for 2 or 3 minutes, until the noodles have absorbed most of the sauce. Serve hot.

INGREDIENT NOTES Bean thread noodles (also called cellophane or glass noodles) are available in most large supermarkets and in Asian groceries. They're made from green mung beans and become glossy and transparent when cooked.

Veggie crumbles are made of textured soy protein and textured wheat protein. Yves Ground Round and Lightlife Smart Ground are brands we recommend. Most packages are 12 ounces, more than this dish requires, but leftovers are good in sautés or in tomato sauce. If you can't find veggie crumbles, substitute grated tofu or seasoned tofu.

serving & menu ideas ∾

Top Jop Chai with chopped scallions and/or toasted sesame seeds and spark things up with Chinese chili paste or chili oil on the side. Kim chee (spicy pickled vegetables), which can be purchased in many supermarkets and Asian specialty shops, is a hassle-free side dish or first course.

spring vegetable sauté ∾

The glistening vegetables in bright shades of green and orange in this garlicky dish are a reminder that summer's just ahead. Frozen shelled edamame (fresh soybeans) are available in natural food stores and many supermarkets. We like to keep a bag on hand to add to soups, stews, and sautés.

SERVES 4

TIME: 35 MINUTES

4 medium carrots

1 bunch of asparagus

1 14-ounce can of artichoke hearts

1 bunch of scallions

2 tablespoons olive oil

4 garlic cloves, minced or pressed

1 teaspoon dried thyme

$1/2$ teaspoon salt

1 tablespoon unbleached white flour

1 cup vegetable broth (see page 295)

2 tablespoons fresh thyme

1 cup frozen shelled edamame (optional)

shaved Parmesan or Pecorino Romano cheese (optional)

Have all of the ingredients prepared and close at hand before you start to sauté. Peel the carrots and cut them in half lengthwise (into quarters if they are very large) and then into $1/2$-inch chunks (about 2 cups). Break off the woody stems of the asparagus, rinse, and cut into pieces about 2 inches long (about 3 cups). Drain the artichoke hearts and cut into quarters. Cut the scallions into inch-long pieces.

Warm the oil in a large skillet on medium-high heat. Add the garlic, dried thyme, and salt and sauté for just half a minute. Stir in the carrots and asparagus and sauté for about 2 minutes. Stir in the artichoke hearts, cover, and simmer on low heat until the vegetables are crisp-tender, about 2 minutes. Using a slotted spoon, lift the vegetables out of the pan juices into a bowl and set aside.

Turn up the heat to high and whisk the flour into the juices in the skillet. Add the vegetable broth and stir until the liquid bubbles and thickens. Add the scallions, edamame, and fresh thyme, and stir in the cooked vegetables. Cook until everything is well coated and hot. Add salt to taste. Serve topped with shaved cheese if you wish.

INGREDIENT NOTES Try green beans instead of asparagus, dried or fresh dill instead of thyme, frozen baby lima beans or peas in place of edamame, baby carrots instead of chopped (pick out uniformly sized ones).

serving & menu ideas ᔚ

Serve on rice, bulghur, or couscous, or in a bowl with bread. A light spring meal like this one deserves Chocolate Ricotta Pudding (page 269) for dessert.

saucy hungarian eggplant ↺

A hearty stew with a robust taste, just right with the nutty flavor of bulghur wheat.

SERVES 4

TIME: 40 MINUTES

1 cup bulghur
¼ teaspoon salt
2 teaspoons olive oil
1½ cups boiling water

1 large onion
3 garlic cloves
1 large eggplant (about 1 pound)
10 ounces cremini mushrooms
1 tablespoon paprika
1 teaspoon dried oregano
¼ teaspoon red pepper flakes
2 tablespoons olive oil
½ teaspoon salt
1 15-ounce can of diced tomatoes
plain yogurt

In a saucepan with a tight-fitting lid, cook the bulghur and salt in the oil on medium heat, stirring constantly, for a couple of minutes to lightly toast the bulghur. Add the boiling water, reduce the heat to low, and cook covered for 10 to 12 minutes, until all the water is absorbed. When the bulghur is done, turn off the heat and let it sit covered until ready to serve.

While the bulghur cooks, prepare the vegetables. Cut the onion into thin slices (about 2 cups). Mince or press the garlic. Cut the unpeeled eggplant into sticks about ½ inch thick and 2 inches long (about 6 cups). Rinse and slice the mushrooms (about 3 cups).

In a large covered pot on medium heat, cook the onion, garlic, paprika, oregano, and red pepper flakes in the oil, stirring often, until the onions soften, about 5 minutes. Add the eggplant, sprinkle with the salt, and cook, stirring constantly, for a minute or two. Add the mushrooms, increase the heat, and continue to cook, stirring frequently, for a couple of minutes. Add the tomatoes, cover, and cook on low heat for about 10 minutes, until the vegetables are tender.

The dish should be saucy but not soupy, so if it's very juicy, increase the heat to high and cook rapidly, stirring often, to reduce the liquid. Serve on the bulghur, topped with yogurt.

serving & menu ideas ∾

This eggplant-mushroom stew is also good served on rice or egg noodles, or in a bowl with plenty of crusty bread. Cherry Shortbread Crumble (page 265) would be the perfect Hungarian-style dessert.

hot & sour stir-fry ∾

Coleslaw mix (shredded cabbage and carrots), one of our favorite simple suppers convenience foods, is available in the produce section of most supermarkets.

SERVES 4

TIME: 25 MINUTES

$1/2$ pound green beans

2 tomatoes

8 ounces coleslaw mix (see page 293) or 4 cups finely shredded cabbage

1 tablespoon grated peeled ginger root

$1^1/2$ teaspoons sugar

$1/2$ teaspoon Chinese chili paste

2 tablespoons soy sauce

1 tablespoon cider vinegar or white vinegar

1 teaspoon cornstarch

1 tablespoon vegetable oil

Have everything prepared and close at hand before you begin to stir-fry. Trim the green beans and cut them in half (about 2 cups). Cut the tomatoes into chunks (about 2 cups). If you don't have coleslaw mix, finely shred cabbage. In a small bowl, combine the ginger, sugar, chili paste, soy sauce, and vinegar, and then stir in the cornstarch and 1 tablespoon of water.

Heat the oil in a wok or large skillet. Add the green beans and stir-fry on high heat for a couple of minutes. Add the cabbage and continue to stir-fry for 2 or 3 minutes. Add the tomatoes and stir-fry until they soften, 2 to 3 minutes. Add the soy sauce-cornstarch mixture and stir-fry for a minute or two, until the sauce thickens and coats the vegetables.

serving & menu ideas ∾

Serve on soba noodles, udon noodles, or rice, and top with Easy Baked Tofu (page 64) or seasoned tofu, or toasted cashews or almonds. How about Lemon Coconut Tapioca Pudding (page 276) or Mango Coconut Sorbet (page 271) for dessert?

curried tofu with tomatoes ∿

Tofu, ever the chameleon, lends itself to pairings with a multi-tude of sauces for nutritious and easily prepared meals. This is a favorite.

SERVES 4

TIME: 30 MINUTES

2 cups chopped onions

1 large red bell pepper, chopped

1 teaspoon salt

2 tablespoons vegetable oil

4 garlic cloves, minced or pressed

$1\frac{1}{2}$ tablespoons grated peeled ginger root

2 tablespoons Curry Powder (page 238) or commercial curry powder or garam masala

$\frac{1}{2}$ teaspoon ground cinnamon

1 cake firm tofu (about 16 ounces), cut into $\frac{1}{2}$-inch cubes

1 28-ounce can of diced tomatoes

black pepper or hot sauce

In a large saucepan with a lid, cook the onions, peppers, and salt in the oil on medium-high heat until softened, about 5 minutes. Add the garlic, ginger, Curry Powder, cinnamon, and tofu. Cover and cook on medium-low heat, stirring frequently, for 5 minutes. Add the tomatoes, cover, and simmer for about 10 minutes to allow the flavors to develop. Occasionally stir gently. Add black pepper or hot sauce to taste.

serving & menu ideas ∿

Serve at the table with pappadams and toasted cashews, chopped cilantro, and plain yogurt. This dish matches well with Coconut Rice (page 182) or Yellow Rice (page 179). Remember to start cooking the rice before you make the curry. If you'd like dessert, Caramel Custard (page 273) is a nice choice.

spicy potatoes & spinach ❧

SERVES 4

TIME: 45 MINUTES

2 tablespoons vegetable oil

1 teaspoon black mustard seeds

1 teaspoon cumin seeds

¹/₂ teaspoon fennel seeds

1 minced fresh chile or ¹/₂ teaspoon red pepper flakes

1¹/₂ cups sliced onions

2 pounds potatoes

1 teaspoon salt

2 cups chopped tomatoes

2 tablespoons lemon juice

10 ounces fresh baby spinach

Heat the oil in a pot on medium-high heat. Add the mustard seeds. When they start to pop, add the cumin and fennel seeds. Stir for a few seconds and add the chile or red pepper flakes and the onions. Lower the heat to medium and cook for about 5 minutes.

Meanwhile, scrub or peel the potatoes and cut them into wedges (about 6 cups). Add the potato wedges, salt, and 1 cup of water to the onions, cover, and cook for about 15 minutes, stirring occasionally, until the potatoes are just tender.

Stir in the tomatoes and lemon juice and cook, covered, until the potatoes are done, about 5 minutes. Add the spinach and simmer until the leaves are wilted.

INGREDIENT NOTES Use ground cumin and/or fennel if seeds aren't available.

In place of fresh tomatoes, you can use a 15-ounce can of diced tomatoes.

serving & menu ideas ❧

Top with yogurt and cilantro. Serve with naan bread or pappadams or on a bed of rice. Serve with chutney or fresh mango slices on the side.

navajo stew ✎

Inspired by a Southwestern Native American dish, this is a sunny, colorful stew of roasted vegetables in a hot and smoky mole-type sauce.

SERVES 4

TIME: 55 MINUTES

2 medium sweet potatoes
2 red or green bell peppers
1 large onion
4 garlic cloves, minced
2 tablespoons vegetable oil
1 tablespoon ground cumin
1 teaspoon salt
¼ teaspoon black pepper
1 15-ounce can of tomatoes
1 tablespoon canned chipotles in adobo sauce (see page 286)
½ cup chopped fresh cilantro
1 15-ounce can of butter beans or black beans, drained
flatbread (tortillas, lavash, or pita)
plain yogurt, sour cream, or Cilantro Yogurt Sauce (page 232)

Preheat the oven to 450°. Lightly oil a baking sheet.

Peel the sweet potatoes and cut into 1-inch cubes. Stem and seed the peppers and cut into 1-inch pieces. Peel the onion and cut it stem end to root end into thin wedges. In a bowl, toss the vegetables with the garlic, oil, cumin, salt, and pepper. Spread on the prepared baking sheet and roast in the oven for about 10 minutes. Stir and continue to roast for another 10 to 15 minutes, until the sweet potatoes are tender but not mushy.

While the vegetables roast, purée the tomatoes, chipotles, and cilantro in a blender until smooth. Set aside. When the vegetables are tender, put them into a 2- to 3-quart baking dish, stir in the tomato-cilantro sauce and the beans, and return to the oven until hot, about 10 minutes.

A few minutes before serving, warm the bread in the oven. Serve the stew in bowls topped with yogurt or sour cream, with warm flatbread on the side.

INGREDIENT NOTE You can substitute 1 tablespoon of Cumin Salt (page 241) for the cumin and salt in the recipe. You may need to add more salt to taste.

serving & menu ideas ∾

This is a filling stew, but Corn on the Cob (page 188) makes a wonderful side dish, and if you've still got room for dessert, consider Warm Plums with Mascarpone (page 262).

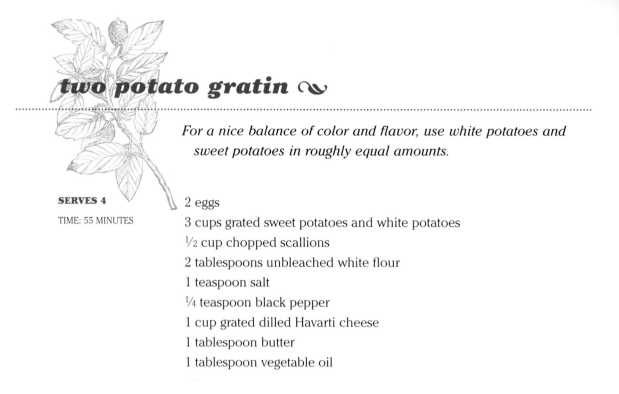

two potato gratin ∾

For a nice balance of color and flavor, use white potatoes and sweet potatoes in roughly equal amounts.

SERVES 4

TIME: 55 MINUTES

2 eggs

3 cups grated sweet potatoes and white potatoes

½ cup chopped scallions

2 tablespoons unbleached white flour

1 teaspoon salt

¼ teaspoon black pepper

1 cup grated dilled Havarti cheese

1 tablespoon butter

1 tablespoon vegetable oil

Preheat the oven to 375°.

Beat the eggs in a large bowl. Add the potatoes, scallions, flour, salt, pepper, and half of the cheese and mix well.

Heat the butter and oil in a large ovenproof skillet (10 to 12 inches) on medium-high heat. Spoon the potato mixture into the skillet and spread evenly. Reduce the heat to medium-low and cook for 10 to 12 minutes, until the bottom is nicely browned. Do not stir.

Transfer the skillet to the oven and bake for about 15 minutes, until the top is golden. Sprinkle the gratin with the remaining cheese and continue to bake until the cheese is melted, about 5 minutes. Cut the gratin into wedges and serve hot.

INGREDIENT NOTE If you don't have dilled Havarti, use Cheddar plus a teaspoon of dried dill or a tablespoon of fresh dill.

serving & menu ideas ∾

We usually serve this with Baked Apples (page 191) and a green salad.

baked stuffed tomatoes ∾

What a versatile dish! You can use almost any kind of cheese (or go vegan—see our suggestions below), and you can add leftover vegetables to the filling. Stuff the tomatoes one day and bake them the next—they're just as tasty!

SERVES 4 TO 6

HANDS-ON TIME:
20 MINUTES

BAKING TIME:
20 TO 25 MINUTES

6 medium tomatoes (about $2\frac{1}{2}$ pounds)

salt and pepper

$2\frac{1}{2}$ cups grated cheese, such as Cheddar, dilled Havarti, or Fontina

$\frac{1}{2}$ cup finely chopped scallions

1 teaspoon dried oregano, dill, or thyme
   (or 1 tablespoon chopped fresh) (optional)

Preheat the oven to 400°.

Cut the tomatoes in half and scoop out the seeds. Oil a baking dish large enough to hold the tomato halves side by side. Place the tomato halves cut-side up in the dish. Sprinkle them with salt and pepper.

In a bowl, combine the cheese, scallions, and herbs. Spoon the filling into the tomato halves. Cover the baking pan with foil and bake for 15 minutes. Uncover and bake until the filling is hot and the cheese is melted, 5 to 10 minutes longer.

variation ∾

To make vegan stuffed tomatoes, use soy or rice cheese. Or use veggie crumbles instead of cheese and add 2 to 3 tablespoons of your favorite brand of barbecue sauce or salsa for flavor.

serving & menu ideas ∾

Excellent served alongside Broccoli Slaw (page 208) or Lemony Green Beans (page 192).

roasted ratatouille ❧

The beauty of this recipe is that the oven does the work while you leisurely prepare a salad and set the table.

SERVES 4

HANDS-ON TIME:
15 TO 20 MINUTES

ROASTING TIME:
35 TO 40 MINUTES

1 zucchini

3 onions

1 eggplant

2 tomatoes

2 red, green, or yellow bell peppers

6 garlic cloves

$\frac{1}{3}$ cup olive oil

1 teaspoon salt

$\frac{1}{2}$ teaspoon black pepper

1 cup packed fresh basil leaves

grated Romano, Pecorino Romano, or Parmesan cheese

Preheat the oven to 450°.

Cut all of the vegetables into 1-inch chunks and place them in a large bowl. (We usually peel the eggplant.) You need between 12 and 14 cups total. Coarsely chop the garlic. Toss the vegetables and garlic with the olive oil, salt, and pepper, and spread on a baking sheet (or two). Roast for 15 minutes and then stir the vegetables. Continue to roast for 25 to 30 minutes, stirring again after 20 minutes, until the vegetables are fork-tender and juicy.

While the vegetables roast, chop the basil. When the vegetables are done, put them in a serving bowl and stir in the chopped basil. Pass the grated cheese at the table.

serving & menu ideas ❧

Start with Baby Greens with Pecans & Pears (page 206). Serve Roasted Ratatouille on Polenta (page 184), couscous, or rice, or with French bread. Leftovers taste even better the next day, packed for lunch or folded into an omelet.

tofu hijiki sauté 〜

This sauté makes an attractive and satisfying supper;
chilled, it makes a delicious side dish or salad.
(See photo on page 34.)

SERVES 4

TIME: 40 MINUTES

1½ cups short-grain brown rice

½ cup dried hijiki seaweed (½ ounce)

1 cake firm tofu (about 16 ounces)

3 cups carrot matchsticks

2 medium onions

2 tablespoons dark sesame oil

2 tablespoons soy sauce

2 tablespoons toasted sesame seeds

In a covered saucepan, bring the rice and 2½ cups of water to a boil. Reduce the heat and simmer covered until the rice is tender and the water absorbed, 35 to 40 minutes.

While the rice cooks, make the sauté. Place the hijiki in a small bowl, add warm water to cover by about an inch, and set aside for 15 minutes. Slice the tofu into bite-sized pieces or strips. Cut the onions into thin slices (2 to 3 cups).

In a large skillet or wok, heat a tablespoon of the sesame oil. Add the tofu and sauté on medium heat, stirring frequently, for several minutes, until browned. Remove the tofu and set aside.

Add the remaining tablespoon of sesame oil to the pan and sauté the onions and carrots until the onions are golden and the carrots are tender, 4 to 5 minutes. Add the drained hijiki, the reserved tofu, and the soy sauce, and cook long enough to heat thoroughly. Stir in the toasted sesame seeds. Serve on the rice.

INGREDIENT NOTES Dried hijiki seaweed is often sold in bulk in natural foods stores, and in many supermarkets it can be found in cellophane packets in the produce section.

Check the produce aisle for bags of matchstick-cut carrots.

roasted vegetable curry ∽

Roasting intensifies the flavors in this fragrant dish, which is easily prepared and requires little attention while it's in the oven. If you like the flavor of garam masala or commercial curry powder and it's in your cupboard, use it.

SERVES 4

HANDS-ON TIME:
20 MINUTES

BAKING TIME:
25 MINUTES

1 large or 2 small sweet potatoes
1 onion
½ small head of cauliflower
2 tablespoons vegetable oil
½ teaspoon salt

CURRY SAUCE
2 teaspoons grated peeled ginger root
2 tablespoons Curry Powder (page 238)
½ teaspoon salt
1 cup coconut milk
1 cup diced tomatoes

Preheat the oven to 450°.

Peel the sweet potatoes and onion, cut them into ¾-inch chunks, and place them in a large bowl. Cut the cauliflower into bite-sized florets (about 3 cups) and add to the bowl. Add the oil, sprinkle with salt, and toss to coat. Spread the vegetables in a single layer on one or two oiled baking trays. Roast for 20 minutes, stirring once after about 10 minutes.

Meanwhile, in a bowl whisk together the ginger, Curry Powder, salt, and coconut milk until smooth. Stir in the tomatoes.

After the vegetables have roasted for 20 minutes, pour the Curry Sauce over them and stir to coat. Return them to the oven until tender, about 5 minutes.

serving & menu ideas ∽

Serve on rice and top with raisins and/or toasted nuts, cooked green peas and chopped cilantro, and a dollop of cool yogurt.

Sesame Tofu with Spinach (page 56)

beans & tofu

sesame tofu with spinach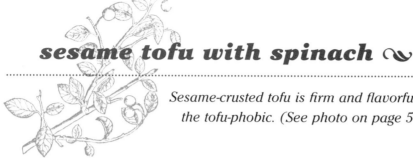

Sesame-crusted tofu is firm and flavorful enough to please even the tofu-phobic. (See photo on page 54.)

SERVES 4

TIME: 30 MINUTES

1 cake firm tofu (about 16 ounces)
¼ cup sesame seeds
2 tablespoons dark sesame oil
2 tablespoons soy sauce
a few drops Tabasco or other hot pepper sauce (optional)
2 teaspoons vegetable oil or olive oil
3 garlic cloves, chopped
10 ounces fresh baby spinach, rinsed
salt and pepper

Slice the block of tofu lengthwise into 4 rectangular slabs. Then slice the slabs in half to make 8 roughly square pieces. Spread the sesame seeds on a plate. Press all of the surfaces of each tofu square into the sesame seeds to coat evenly.

Heat the sesame oil in a large skillet on medium heat. Arrange the tofu squares in a single layer in the skillet and cook for about 5 minutes. With a spatula, carefully turn them over and cook for about 5 minutes on the other side. Add the soy sauce and Tabasco, turn the tofu squares over, and cook for another minute, until most of the liquid is absorbed. Transfer the tofu squares to a plate. (Leave stray sesame seeds in the pan.)

Add the oil and the garlic to the skillet and sauté for about 30 seconds, until golden. Add the still damp rinsed spinach and cook for a minute or two, stirring constantly, until wilted but still bright green. Season with salt and pepper.

Place the spinach on a platter and top with the tofu.

serving & menu ideas

Serve with rice, soba noodles, orzo, or Roasted Sweet Potatoes (page 197). Indulge in Butterscotch Icebox Cookies (page 279) for dessert.

green & white bean gratin ∾

This creamy, cold-weather casserole with a golden, crunchy topping can be assembled ahead and baked when you're ready.

SERVES 4 TO 6

HANDS-ON TIME:
20 MINUTES

BAKING TIME:
35 MINUTES

2 cups frozen cut green beans

2 15-ounce cans of white beans

4 garlic cloves, chopped

2 teaspoons dried rosemary, sage, or thyme

¼ teaspoon salt

pinch of black pepper

1 cup grated Cheddar, Fontina, or Gruyère cheese

1 cup bread crumbs

1 cup grated Parmesan cheese

2 tablespoons melted butter

Preheat the oven to 375°. Butter an 8-inch square baking dish. Defrost the green beans by placing them in very hot water for a few minutes. Drain and spread to cover the bottom of the prepared baking dish.

In a blender, whirl one can of white beans, undrained, with the garlic, herbs, salt, and pepper until smooth. Pour over the green beans in the baking dish and sprinkle with the Cheddar cheese. Drain the second can of white beans and spread the beans on top.

In a small bowl, combine the bread crumbs, Parmesan, and melted butter. Sprinkle over the top of the gratin. Bake covered for 25 minutes. Uncover and bake until golden and bubbling, about 10 minutes more.

INGREDIENT NOTE You can substitute fresh green beans that have been stemmed, cut into 2-inch lengths, and blanched, if you prefer.

serving & menu ideas ∾

On the side, try Apples Two Ways (page 191) or Carrot Salad with Raspberry Vinaigrette (page 217). A simple, not-too-rich dessert, such as Riesling Roasted Pears (page 264) or Mocha Sorbet (page 272) would be just right.

black beans with pickled red onions ∽

Black beans and rice with an interesting twist: fuchsia-colored pickled red onions. Make extra! They're a flavorful condiment for sandwiches, soups, and salads, and they keep in the refrigerator for several weeks.

SERVES 4

TIME: 35 MINUTES

Yellow Rice (page 179)

PICKLED RED ONIONS

2 large red onions

3 cups boiling water

1 teaspoon salt

1 teaspoon sugar

1/4 teaspoon ground allspice

1 tablespoon vinegar

1/4 cup fresh lime juice

1 teaspoon Tabasco or other hot pepper sauce (optional)

SEASONED BLACK BEANS

1 tablespoon olive oil

2 garlic cloves, minced or pressed

1 teaspoon ground cumin

1 1/2 teaspoons dried oregano

2 15-ounce cans of black beans, undrained

1/4 cup chopped fresh cilantro

Prepare the Yellow Rice.

While the rice cooks, slice the onions into rings. In a heatproof bowl, cover the onions with the boiling water and set aside for 10 minutes. In a separate bowl, combine the salt, sugar, allspice, vinegar, lime juice, and Tabasco. Drain the onions. Combine the drained onions and the pickling ingredients and mix well. Set aside.

For the beans, warm the oil in a saucepan on medium heat and then add the garlic, cumin, and oregano. Cook for just a minute and then add the beans. Simmer for 5 to 8 minutes, until the beans are heated through and have absorbed the seasonings. Stir in the cilantro.

Serve the rice topped with beans and pickled onions.

serving & menu ideas ∾

Toss a green salad with Cilantro Lime Dressing (page 225) and enjoy Caramel Custard (page 273) for dessert. Try the beans and rice topped with Quick Avocado & Corn Salsa (page 233) instead of the pickled onions.

shortcut chili ∾

There must be as many recipes for chili as there are cooks. This one has the surprising addition of lentils and the smoky spiciness of chipotles.

SERVES 4 TO 6

TIME: 25 MINUTES

2 cups chopped onions

3 garlic cloves, minced or pressed

1 teaspoon salt

2 tablespoons olive oil

1 tablespoon minced canned chipotles in adobo sauce (see page 286)

1 red or green bell pepper, diced

1 15-ounce can of red kidney beans, drained

1 15-ounce can of lentils, undrained

1 15-ounce can of diced tomatoes

1 tablespoon minced fresh cilantro

sour cream (optional)

In a soup pot, sauté the onions, garlic, and salt in the oil until soft, 5 to 10 minutes.

Add the chipotles and the bell peppers, cover, and cook for 2 minutes. Stir in the beans, lentils, and tomatoes. Cover and simmer on low heat for 5 to 10 minutes or until everything is hot. Stir in the cilantro. Serve topped with sour cream, if you wish.

INGREDIENT NOTE In addition to or in place of the chipotles, add 2 teaspoons Chili Powder (page 235).

serving & menu ideas ∾

Serve spooned over Polenta (page 184) or Yellow Rice (page 179), or with cornbread or tortilla chips. Then cool your palate with Mango Coconut Sorbet (page 271).

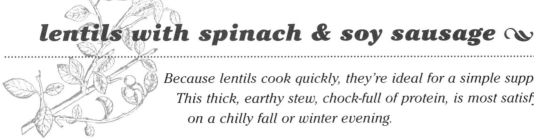

lentils with spinach & soy sausage ᘒ

Because lentils cook quickly, they're ideal for a simple supper. This thick, earthy stew, chock-full of protein, is most satisfying on a chilly fall or winter evening.

SERVES 4

TIME: 40 MINUTES

4 garlic cloves, minced
2 teaspoons ground coriander
1 tablespoon olive oil
1 quart vegetable broth (see page 295)
2 bay leaves
1 cup green or brown lentils
2 cups diced potatoes
8 ounces soy sausage links
2 teaspoons olive oil
4 cups fresh baby spinach (about 5 ounces)
salt and pepper
grated Cheddar or crumbled feta cheese or ricotta salata

In a soup pot, cook the garlic and coriander in the olive oil for a minute. Add the broth, bay leaves, and lentils, cover, and bring to a boil. Reduce the heat to a simmer and cook covered for 10 minutes.

Add the potatoes, cover, and cook until the potatoes are tender and the lentils are soft, about 15 minutes.

While the lentils and potatoes cook, cut the soy sausage into $1/2$ inch-thick rounds. In a skillet on medium-low heat, cook the rounds in the olive oil, turning frequently, until browned, 5 or 10 minutes. Rinse, drain, and chop the spinach.

When the lentils and potatoes are done, add the sausage and spinach and stir until the spinach is just wilted but still bright green, about a minute. Add salt and pepper to taste. Serve topped with cheese.

nachos grandes ࿇

Is this really dinner? It is casual, messy finger food, but it has beans, grain, and cheese, it's quite filling, and kids love it. We like Cheddar, Monterey Jack, or Mexican cheeses such asadero and queso quesadilla for this recipe.

SERVES 4

TIME: 20 MINUTES

4 cups corn tortilla chips

1 15-ounce can of refried beans

1½ cups diced tomatoes

1 tablespoon minced canned or fresh chiles, or more to taste (optional)

¼ cup sliced black or green olives

½ cup of your favorite salsa

¼ cup sour cream

6 ounces shredded cheese (about 2 cups)

2 tablespoons minced scallions

Preheat the oven to 400°. Choose a baking dish about 9 x 13 inches, with 2 inch-high sides.

Layer all of the ingredients in the baking dish in the order given above. If the refried beans are too stiff to easily spoon over the chips, thin them with a little water.

Bake for about 15 minutes, until the beans in the center are steaming hot and the cheese is melted and bubbling.

variations ࿇

Add corn kernels, shredded zucchini, chopped pimientos, or chopped cilantro to the assembly.

serving & menu ideas ࿇

Serve with Broccoli Slaw (page 208) or avocado slices. Top off this fun simple supper with a 5-Minute Milkshake (page 281).

easy baked tofu ❧

We think that this may be the most useful recipe in the book. Baked tofu is a reliable standby and can be dressed up to suit almost any menu. Whip up a marinade, pop the tofu in the oven, start cooking rice or pasta, and decide on a vegetable or salad. Baked tofu is also a nice addition to stews, sautés, sandwiches, and salads.

SERVES 4

1 cake firm tofu (about 16 ounces)

BASIC MARINADE
1 tablespoon vegetable oil
1 tablespoon dark sesame oil
3 tablespoons soy sauce
2 teaspoons grated peeled ginger root (optional)
1 garlic clove, pressed (optional)

IN THE OVEN:
HANDS-ON TIME: 5 TO 10 MINUTES
BAKING TIME: 30 TO 40 MINUTES

Preheat the oven to 400°. Cut the tofu into slices, cubes, triangles, or sticks. Lightly oil a baking dish large enough to hold the tofu in a single layer. Whisk together the marinade ingredients (or variation ingredients, if using) and drizzle over the tofu. Gently turn or toss to coat thoroughly. Bake uncovered, stirring once or twice, until the oil is sizzling and the tofu is firm and chewy, 30 to 40 minutes. Serve hot, at room temperature, or chilled.

ON THE STOVETOP:
TIME: 15 MINUTES

Cut the tofu into small cubes. Heat the vegetable oil and the sesame oil in a large skillet. Add the tofu and sauté, stirring often, for 4 or 5 minutes, until lightly golden. Add the soy sauce (and other marinade ingredients if you are using a variation), lower the heat, and simmer for 3 or 4 minutes longer. Done!

....

SPICY TOFU Add 2 to 3 teaspoons of Chinese chili paste with garlic to the basic marinade and reduce the soy sauce to 2 tablespoons.

Serve with assorted steamed and raw vegetables and Spicy Peanut Sauce (page 256).

SWEET & SOUR TOFU Add 2 tablespoons of vinegar and 1 tablespoon of honey, maple syrup, or sugar to the basic marinade.

Serve with Lemongrass Rice (page 181) and Sesame Broccoli (page 193).

CHIPOTLE TOFU Use 2 tablespoons vegetable oil, 2 tablespoons soy sauce, 2 tablespoons chopped chipotles in adobo sauce, and ¼ cup chopped fresh cilantro (optional) for the marinade.

Try with Yellow Rice (page 179) and Quick Avocado & Corn Salsa (page 233).

BARBECUE TOFU Mix together 1 tablespoon vegetable oil, 1 tablespoon soy sauce, and ¾ cup of barbecue sauce.

Serve on rice, orzo, or mashed potatoes topped with sautéed onions and peppers. On the side, serve collards (page 162) and/or Baked Acorn Squash Crescents (page 198).

SOUTHERN-STYLE TOFU Coat the tofu with a mixture of 1 tablespoon vegetable oil and 1 tablespoon Old Bay Seasoning.

Bring on the backyard picnic food—Chipotle Potato Salad (page 216), corn on the cob with one of our festive toppings (page 188), Broccoli Slaw (page 208), and Banana Cupcakes (page 274).

scrambled tofu with greens & raspberry chipotle sauce ∽

You can make the sauce with other fruit spreads, such as peach, apricot, or strawberry. Make extra sauce—it will keep in the refrigerator for several weeks.

SERVES 3 OR 4

TIME: 30 MINUTES

2 tablespoons vegetable oil

1 cup chopped onions

3 garlic cloves, chopped

3 cups chopped kale, chard, or collards, rinsed and lightly drained

1 cake firm tofu (about 16 ounces)

3 tablespoons soy sauce

RASPBERRY CHIPOTLE SAUCE

1/3 cup raspberry fruit spread or jam

2 teaspoons minced canned chipotles in adobo sauce
   (see page 286)

1 to 3 teaspoons lemon juice

Heat the oil in a large skillet on medium heat. Sauté the onions in the oil for a couple of minutes, until they begin to soften. Add the garlic and cook for another minute. Stir in the greens, cover, and steam until the greens begin to wilt.

While the greens steam, in a bowl, use a fork to mash the tofu with the soy sauce. Uncover the skillet, increase the heat to high, and cook off any remaining water. Stir in the mashed tofu and cook for 3 or 4 minutes. With a spatula, turn over the tofu mixture and cook for another 3 or 4 minutes, until the tofu just begins to brown.

While the tofu cooks, make the Raspberry Chipotle Sauce. In a small saucepan, stir together the fruit spread, chipotles, and 2 tablespoons of water. Simmer on low heat for about 2 minutes, until hot and saucy. Stir in 1 teaspoon of lemon juice. Add more water if the sauce is too thick. Add more lemon juice to taste.

Serve the scrambled tofu topped with the sauce.

serving & menu ideas ∽

Serve with toast or on plain rice, Yellow Rice (page 179), or Green Rice (page 180).

lemon herb tofu ∾

....

This delightfully tangy tofu pairs especially well with Greek or
Italian dishes.

SERVES 4

HANDS-ON TIME:
10 TO 15 MINUTES

BAKING TIME:
30 TO 35 MINUTES

1 cake firm tofu (about 16 ounces)

¼ cup lemon juice

3 tablespoons soy sauce

2 tablespoons olive oil

2 teaspoons dried herbs, such as rosemary, dill, or oregano

¼ teaspoon black pepper

2 garlic cloves, minced (optional)

Preheat the oven to 400°. Cut the block of tofu into 4 slices and then cut the slices into cubes, triangles, or strips. Spread the tofu pieces in a single layer in a lightly oiled baking pan large enough to hold them.

Whisk together the lemon juice, soy sauce, oil, herbs, pepper, and garlic, and pour over the tofu. Bake uncovered, stirring every 10 or 15 minutes, until most of the marinade is absorbed, the oil is sizzling, and the tofu is firm and chewy, 30 to 35 minutes. Serve hot, at room temperature, or chilled.

INGREDIENT NOTE Use fresh herbs in place of dried: ¼ cup chopped fresh dill or cilantro, 2 tablespoons chopped fresh oregano, or 1 tablespoon chopped fresh rosemary.

serving & menu ideas ∾
....

Try this tofu on Greek Salad (page 211), or create a Mediterranean plate with Tomatoes & Onions with Mint (page 205) and steamed artichokes with Herbed Aioli (page 224).

west indian red beans & coconut rice ✎

In the Caribbean, red beans and rice are cooked together, but at Moosewood we like to ladle saucy red beans over a bed of fragrant coconut rice and garnish with a little greenery.

SERVES 4 TO 6

TIME: 35 MINUTES

Coconut Rice (page 182)
1½ cups diced onions
1 tablespoon vegetable oil
½ teaspoon red pepper flakes or 1 fresh chile, minced
salt
½ teaspoon dried thyme
¼ teaspoon allspice
1 28-ounce can of diced tomatoes
1 28-ounce can of red kidney beans, drained
chopped scallions and/or cilantro

Cook the Coconut Rice.

While the rice is cooking, in a saucepan on medium heat, sauté the onions in the oil for 3 or 4 minutes. Add the red pepper flakes, sprinkle lightly with salt, cover, and cook, stirring occasionally, until the onions are soft, 5 to 8 minutes. Add the thyme, allspice, tomatoes, and beans, cover, and simmer for 10 to 15 minutes, stirring occasionally.

Serve the red beans on a bed of the rice and top with scallions and/or cilantro.

serving & menu ideas ✎

Delicious with a side of collards (page 162) or avocado and mango slices. Save room for Caribbean Sautéed Bananas (page 263).

tofu & mushrooms marsala ❧

We think this inventive adaptation of a classic Italian dish is so good that it will soon show up on menus in the old neighborhoods. You never know.

SERVES 4

TIME: 30 MINUTES

4 garlic cloves, pressed or minced

2 tablespoons olive oil

1 red bell pepper, chopped

$\frac{1}{2}$ teaspoon dried oregano

$\frac{1}{2}$ teaspoon salt

2 cups Marsala wine

1 cake firm tofu (about 16 ounces), cut into $\frac{3}{4}$-inch cubes

10 ounces moonlight or cremini mushrooms, sliced

1 14-ounce can of diced tomatoes

$\frac{1}{4}$ cup chopped fresh basil

salt and pepper

1 loaf of crusty bread

In a pot on medium heat, cook the garlic in the oil just until it sizzles and then add the bell peppers, oregano, and salt. Cook, stirring often, for 5 minutes. Add the Marsala and the tofu and cook on high heat for 4 minutes to reduce the wine a bit. Add the mushrooms and tomatoes and cook on medium-high heat for 5 minutes. Add the basil and salt and pepper to taste.

Serve with plenty of crusty bread to soak up the flavorful broth.

serving & menu ideas ❧

On the side, Lemony Green Beans (page 192) and/or a green salad with Sour Cream Lemon Dressing (page 223), and Orange-Almond Polenta Cake (page 266) for dessert.

sichuan silken tofu

*Why order takeout when you can create classic Chinese flavors
so easily at home?*

SERVES 2 TO 3

TIME: 20 MINUTES

1 cake silken or soft tofu (about 16 ounces)

3 scallions

1 cup water

1 tablespoon cornstarch

½ teaspoon salt

1 teaspoon soy sauce

½ teaspoon dark sesame oil

¼ teaspoon sugar

½ teaspoon rice vinegar, cider vinegar, or white vinegar

1 teaspoon peanut oil or vegetable oil

½ teaspoon Chinese chili paste

½ cup sliced snow peas or frozen green peas (optional)

Cut the tofu into 1-inch cubes and set aside. Chop the scallions (about ½ cup). In a
bowl, whisk the water, cornstarch, salt, soy sauce, sesame oil, sugar, and vinegar until
well blended.

Warm a skillet or saucepan on medium-high heat. When the pan is hot, add the oil and
then the chili paste, sizzle for a few seconds, and then stir in the cornstarch-water mixture. Stir until the sauce simmers and thickens, about 2 minutes. Add the chopped scallions and the peas, if using. Gently stir in the tofu cubes and cook until heated through.

INGREDIENT NOTE Silken tofu gives this dish a custardy consistency that some of us really
like, but it's a little bit tricky to work with. It's slippery and hard to cut into neat cubes,
so don't worry if some fall apart. Soft tofu is a little easier to cut into cubes, and some
people prefer the texture.

serving & menu ideas

Serve the tofu on a bed of rice or udon noodles, with Pan-Asian Slaw (page 212) or a
steamed green vegetable on the side.

white bean & mushroom ragout ∾

Beans and mushrooms are a great combo and quintessentially Italian. Experiment with different varieties and colors of beans.

SERVES 4

TIME: 35 MINUTES

1½ tablespoons olive oil
1½ cups finely chopped onions
2 garlic cloves, minced
1 teaspoon dried thyme, rosemary, or sage
1 teaspoon ground fennel seeds (optional)
10 ounces moonlight or cremini mushrooms
¼ cup dry red or white wine
1 15-ounce can of cannellini beans, drained
1 28-ounce can of diced tomatoes
½ cup chopped fresh parsley or basil
salt and pepper
Polenta (page 184)
grated Parmesan cheese (optional)

In a saucepan on medium heat, warm the oil and add the onions, garlic, herbs, and fennel. Sprinkle lightly with salt, cover, and cook, stirring occasionally, for 8 to 10 minutes, until the onions are softened and starting to brown. While the onions cook, rinse and quarter the mushrooms (about 3 cups).

When the onions are soft, stir in the mushrooms and wine, cover, and simmer for 5 minutes. Stir in the beans, tomatoes, and parsley, cover, and bring to a simmer. Cook for about 10 minutes, until hot and juicy, stirring occasionally. Add salt and pepper to taste.

While the ragout simmers, prepare the Polenta.

Serve the ragout on the Polenta and sprinkle with cheese if you like.

serving & menu ideas ∾

You could serve the ragout on orzo or any small pasta or in a bowl with plenty of crusty bread. A crisp green salad is a welcome counterpoint to the soft ragout and polenta. How about one of the easy Fruit & Cheese Plates (page 260) for dessert?

Veggie Western Omelet (page 76)

egg dishes

veggie western omelet ∾

Serve this right out of the pan for a quick home-style meal. Warm,
at room temperature, or straight from the fridge, this omelet
also makes a great sandwich with mayonnaise and tomato.
(See photo on page 74.)

SERVES 2

TIME: 20 MINUTES

2 teaspoons olive oil

1 cup diced red onions

2 cups diced bell peppers

4 eggs

¼ teaspoon salt

sprinkling of black pepper

In a 10-inch skillet on medium-high heat, cook the onions and peppers in the oil, stirring frequently, until the onions soften but the peppers are still firm, about 7 minutes.

In a bowl, beat the eggs, a tablespoon of water, and the salt and pepper with a fork until frothy. Slowly pour the eggs over the peppers and onions. Lower the heat and cook for 3 or 4 minutes, until the eggs are set and beginning to brown on the bottom. With the edge of a spatula, cut the omelet into 4 wedges. Turn the wedges over and cook on the second side for a minute or two, until browned. (If you use a nonstick skillet, you may be able to flip the whole thing.) Serve hot or at room temperature.

variation ∾

Add cheese: Cheddar, a smoked cheese, or feta.

serving & menu ideas ∾

Serve with Tomato Tortilla Soup (page 117), or top the omelet with your favorite tomato salsa or sliced tomatoes and serve with toast or cheese grits (page 162).

collegetown eggs ⌒

One of our favorite home-style dishes at Hong Kong Restaurant in Ithaca's Collegetown, this is the Chinese version of scrambled eggs and ketchup!

SERVES 2

TIME: 10 MINUTES

1 tomato
1/8 teaspoon dark sesame oil
salt and pepper
2 scallions
3 eggs
1/4 teaspoon sugar
2 teaspoons vegetable oil

Cut the tomato into wedges. In a small bowl, gently toss the wedges with the sesame oil and a sprinkling of salt and pepper. Chop the scallions and place them in a separate bowl with the eggs, sugar, a teaspoon of water, and a dash of salt and pepper. Beat until foamy.

In a small skillet on medium-high heat, warm the oil. Pour in the egg mixture and turn the heat down to medium. In about a minute, when the eggs have begun to set, with a spatula, gently push the eggs from the outside of the pan toward the center. After about a minute, flip the eggs to cook the other side. As soon as the eggs are fully set, remove from the heat.

Divide the eggs between two plates and top with the tomatoes.

serving & menu ideas ⌒

For a heartier meal, serve with rice or toast and Pan-Asian Slaw (page 212).

greek frittata

If you love spinach and feta, this simple supper is for you.

SERVES 2

TIME: 20 MINUTES

½ cup chopped scallions

2 garlic cloves, minced

1 tablespoon olive oil

2 cups packed fresh baby spinach

½ teaspoon dried oregano or dill (1 teaspoon chopped fresh)

4 eggs

dashes of salt and pepper

1 small tomato, chopped

½ cup crumbled feta cheese

In a large skillet on medium-low heat, cook the scallions and garlic in the oil for a couple of minutes. Add the spinach and the herbs if using dried. Cook uncovered for 3 or 4 minutes, until the spinach is wilted.

In a bowl, beat the eggs, a tablespoon of water, herbs if using fresh, and salt and pepper. Pour the eggs over the spinach. When the eggs begin to set, use a spatula to cut through to the bottom in a couple of places in the center of the frittata and lift the cooked edges while you tilt the pan so the raw egg runs onto the hot skillet.

When the eggs are mostly set, spread the tomatoes and feta evenly over the top. Lower the heat and cover for a minute or two until the tomatoes are hot, the feta is soft and melty, and the eggs are fully set.

serving & menu ideas ∽

This frittata is great simply with buttered toast. Potatoes with Lemon & Capers (page 195) is delicious alongside, and of course, you can't go wrong with a Greek Salad (page 211).

poached huevos rancheros ॐ

This might be just the ticket when you're looking for something tasty and really fast.

SERVES 2

TIME: 10 MINUTES

2 cups of your favorite salsa or Blender Tomato
   Hot Sauce (page 244)
4 eggs
4 tortillas (corn or flour)
1⅓ cups grated Monterey Jack or Cheddar cheese

Pour the salsa into a lightly oiled medium skillet and bring it to a simmer. Make four wells in the salsa and break an egg (being careful not to break the yolk) into each one. Reduce the heat to low, cover, and poach the eggs for about 3 minutes. Meanwhile, warm the tortillas in a dry skillet on the stovetop.

Remove the skillet with the poached eggs from the heat, sprinkle the cheese on top, cover, and let sit long enough to melt the cheese. Transfer each egg, with a scoop of salsa, onto one of the warm tortillas and serve right away.

serving & menu ideas ॐ

Serve with a tossed green salad topped with avocado slices and Cilantro Lime Dressing (page 225) or with refried beans or Corn on the Cob (page 188), and cantaloupe.

tunisian potato omelet ⌒

In this delicious omelet, we borrowed the taste of garlic, caraway, and coriander from harissa, *the classic Tunisian seasoning. The omelet can also be cut into wedges and served as an appetizer or as part of a tapas or antipasto platter.*

SERVES 4

TIME: 45 MINUTES

SPICY TOMATO SAUCE

1 tablespoon vegetable oil or olive oil

4 garlic cloves, minced

$\frac{1}{2}$ to 1 teaspoon red pepper flakes

$\frac{1}{4}$ teaspoon salt

1 teaspoon ground caraway

1 teaspoon ground coriander

1 15-ounce can of diced tomatoes

POTATO OMELET

2 tablespoons olive oil

1$\frac{1}{2}$ cups diced onions

1 teaspoon salt

2 teaspoons ground caraway

2 teaspoons ground coriander

2 cups diced potatoes

6 eggs

$\frac{1}{2}$ cup grated Parmesan or Pecorino Romano cheese

Make the Spicy Tomato Sauce: Warm the oil in a small saucepan. Sizzle the garlic in the oil for a few seconds. Add the pepper flakes, salt, caraway, and coriander and cook briefly, about 30 seconds. Add the tomatoes and bring to a simmer. Simmer on low heat, stirring occasionally, while you prepare the omelet.

For the omelet, warm the oil in a large well-seasoned or nonstick skillet, add the onions, and cook on medium-high heat for about 3 minutes, until they soften and begin to turn translucent. Stir in the salt, caraway, coriander, and potatoes and cook for about a minute. Add ¼ cup of water, cover, and cook on medium-low heat until the potatoes are tender, 10 to 15 minutes. Stir often and check for sticking; add more water if necessary.

While the potatoes cook, in a bowl, beat the eggs with 2 tablespoons of water. When the potatoes are tender, pour the eggs over them and cook on medium-low heat. When the eggs begin to set, lift the cooked edges while you tilt the pan so the uncooked egg slips under, onto the hot skillet. Sprinkle on cheese, cover, and cook on low heat until the eggs are set and the cheese is melted.

Divide the omelet into quarters. Serve hot, cold, or at room temperature, topped with Spicy Tomato Sauce.

serving & menu ideas ∾
....
Baby Greens with Pecans & Pears (page 206) complements the spiciness of the sauce. Serve creamy Lemon Coconut Tapioca Pudding (page 276) for dessert.

savory bread & cheese bake ∾

This golden pudding sends out a wonderfully appetizing aroma as it bakes. You can keep it unbaked in the refrigerator for up to a day—just allow for more baking time.

SERVES 4 TO 6

HANDS-ON TIME:
15 TO 20 MINUTES

BAKING TIME:
30 TO 35 MINUTES

3 tablespoons butter

12 ounces crusty bread (French, Italian, or sourdough)

1 cup grated cheese, such as Cheddar, Swiss, or Monterey Jack

1 cup chopped scallions

6 eggs

2 cups milk

1 teaspoon salt

¼ teaspoon black pepper

1 generous tablespoon Dijon mustard

Preheat the oven to 375°. Put the butter in a 2-quart baking dish and place in the oven to melt. When the butter is melted, swirl it around to coat the dish. While the butter melts, cut the bread into 1-inch cubes (about 6 cups, loosely packed). Place the bread cubes in the buttered baking dish. Sprinkle evenly with the cheese and scallions.

Purée the eggs, milk, salt, pepper, and mustard in a blender, or beat the eggs in a bowl and then whisk in the other ingredients. Pour the custard over the bread and use a spatula to push the bread down into the custard. Bake covered with aluminum foil for 25 to 30 minutes (depending on the shape and depth of the baking dish). Remove the foil and bake until puffy and golden brown, about 5 minutes.

INGREDIENT NOTE This recipe provides a great way to use up stale, dry bread. It is also good made with rye, pumpernickel, or whole wheat bread.

serving & menu ideas ∾

Serve with Broccoli Tomato Salad (page 204), or, as long as your oven is on, roast cauliflower and red peppers that you've tossed with olive oil and Cumin Salt (page 241) or Moroccan Spice Mix (page 239).

chipotle scrambled eggs ↬

Fast, easy, warm, and inviting, this dish will quickly become a favorite part of your simple supper repertoire.

SERVES 2 OR 3

TIME: 15 MINUTES

½ cup minced onions

1 tablespoon vegetable oil or butter

6 eggs

1 tablespoon minced canned chipotles in adobo sauce
   (see page 286)

salt and pepper

1 ounce cream cheese, cut into small pieces,
   or ¼ cup grated Monterey Jack cheese

In a large skillet on medium heat, cook the onions in the oil or butter until golden, about 4 minutes.

In a bowl, beat the eggs with the chipotles and adobo sauce and a sprinkling of salt and pepper. Add to the skillet and cook, stirring to scramble, until the eggs are nearly set. Sprinkle the cheese evenly over the eggs. Reduce the heat to low and cover the skillet until the cheese melts, about a minute.

variation ↬

Chipotle Scrambled Eggs make a great huevos rancheros–style quesadilla. When cooking the eggs, place a tortilla on top of them in the pan while they're still a little wet. When the eggs are cooked, flip them over so the tortilla is on the pan with egg on top. (You might need 2 spatulas.) Sprinkle on some cheese and salsa, and top with a second tortilla. When the cheese is melted, flip the quesadilla over to brown the top tortilla. Cut into wedges.

serving & menu ideas ↬

Serve with tomato and avocado slices dressed with Cilantro Lime Dressing (page 225).

egg foo yung omelet ∾

Try this versatile omelet with traditional ingredients such as bean sprouts or water chestnuts, or look in your vegetable crisper and use that lonely stalk of celery or leftover carrot half, a handful of mushrooms or snow peas, some broccoli florets, etc. Try for a variety of colors and use up to 2 cups of chopped vegetables.

SERVES 2

TIME: 20 MINUTES

1 tablespoon vegetable oil

$\frac{1}{2}$ cup thinly sliced onions or chopped scallions

1 cup sliced bok choy or cabbage

$\frac{1}{2}$ cup thinly sliced red bell peppers

4 eggs

1 teaspoon soy sauce

1 teaspoon peeled and grated ginger root

SAUCE

1 tablespoon cornstarch

1 tablespoon soy sauce

a few drops of dark sesame oil

In an 8- to 10-inch skillet on medium heat, warm the oil. Add the onions or scallions, bok choy or cabbage, and peppers, cover, and cook until tender, about 7 minutes.

While the vegetables cook, in a bowl, whisk the eggs with the soy sauce, ginger, and a tablespoon of water. Make the sauce in a small saucepan: Whisk the cornstarch into 1 cup of water. Add the soy sauce and sesame oil. Bring to a boil on high heat, stirring often. Reduce the heat and simmer, stirring constantly until the sauce is clear and thickened. Set aside.

Stir the vegetables in the skillet and add additional oil if necessary to prevent sticking. Pour the beaten eggs over the vegetables, lower the heat, cover, and cook until the eggs are set, about 5 minutes.

Fold the omelet in half and serve topped with the sauce.

Spinach Polenta (page 93)

main dish grains

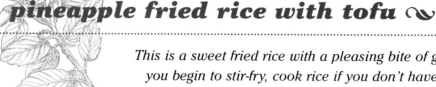

pineapple fried rice with tofu ↜

This is a sweet fried rice with a pleasing bite of ginger. Before you begin to stir-fry, cook rice if you don't have any left over, and have everything prepped and close at hand.

SERVES 4

TIME: 30 MINUTES

½ cake firm tofu (about 8 ounces)

⅓ cup soy sauce

1 teaspoon dark sesame oil

3 tablespoons vegetable oil

3 garlic cloves, minced or pressed

1 tablespoon grated peeled ginger root

½ teaspoon Chinese chili paste (optional)

1 red or orange bell pepper, diced

1 stalk celery, diced

2 scallions, minced

1 20-ounce can of unsweetened pineapple chunks, drained,
     or 2 cups fresh pineapple chunks

4 cups cooked jasmine, sushi, or brown rice

toasted cashews

Cut the tofu into ½-inch cubes and place them in a bowl. Pour the soy sauce and sesame oil over the cubes and stir gently. Set aside.

In a wok or large skillet, heat the vegetable oil. Add the garlic, ginger, and chili paste and stir-fry on medium heat for a minute. Add the peppers, celery, scallions, and the tofu with the marinade, and continue to stir-fry until the vegetables are tender, about 5 minutes. Add the pineapple and rice and stir-fry until the rice is hot, about 3 minutes. Serve topped with toasted cashews.

serving & menu ideas ↜

This spicy-sweet fried rice is enough, but if you want a side dish, choose Sesame Broccoli (page 193). Pass a plate of Butterscotch Icebox Cookies (page 279) for dessert.

beans & greens risotto ∾

Beans, grains, vegetables, cheese—this
healthy, hearty dish has it all.

SERVES 4

TIME: 40 MINUTES

1 quart vegetable broth (see page 295)
1 15-ounce can of diced tomatoes
4 garlic cloves, minced or pressed
1 tablespoon olive oil
1½ cups arborio rice
1 15-ounce can of small red beans or pinto beans, drained
1 small head escarole, chopped (about 3 cups)
¼ cup grated Pecorino Romano or Parmesan cheese
salt and pepper
lemon wedges (optional)

In a saucepan, bring the broth and tomatoes to a boil and then reduce the heat to maintain a gentle simmer.

Meanwhile, in a large, heavy saucepan on medium-high heat, cook the garlic in the oil until just golden, a few seconds. Add the rice and stir until the grains are well coated with oil. Ladle in the hot broth and tomatoes a cup at a time, stirring often. After each addition, let the rice absorb most of the broth before adding more. Add the beans with the last cup of broth.

When most of the broth is absorbed and the rice is tender but still al dente, stir in the escarole, in batches if necessary, until it wilts but is still bright green. Stir in the cheese and season with salt and pepper. Serve hot, with wedges of lemon if you wish.

serving & menu ideas ∾

A crisp, cold fruit salad is a good accompaniment for this simple supper. Or try one of our Two Sweet Sauces (page 280) on vanilla ice cream.

rarebit risotto ~

Beer and Cheddar aren't typical ingredients for risotto, but this dish sure is good!

SERVES 4

TIME: 40 MINUTES

1 quart vegetable broth (see page 295)
1 tablespoon olive oil
1½ cups arborio rice
12 ounces beer (1½ cups)
3 cups chopped broccoli
1 tablespoon Dijon mustard
4 cups loosely packed grated sharp Cheddar cheese
    (about 10 ounces)
2 cups chopped tomatoes or halved cherry tomatoes
sprinkling of black pepper

In a saucepan, bring the broth to a boil and then reduce the heat to maintain a gentle simmer.

Meanwhile, in a large, heavy saucepan on medium-high heat, warm the olive oil. Add the rice and stir until well coated with oil. Add the beer and stir until the rice has absorbed the liquid, a couple of minutes. Ladle in the simmering broth a cup at a time, stirring often. Let the rice absorb most of the broth before adding the next cup, usually about 5 minutes between additions.

While the risotto is cooking, steam the broccoli until bright green and just tender. Set aside.

When the last of the broth is absorbed, the kernels of rice should be al dente and the risotto moist. Add the mustard and cheese to the risotto and stir until the cheese is melted. Stir in the broccoli and tomatoes, season with black pepper, and serve hot.

serving & menu ideas ~

Serve something crisp with this silky risotto.

spinach artichoke risotto ⌀

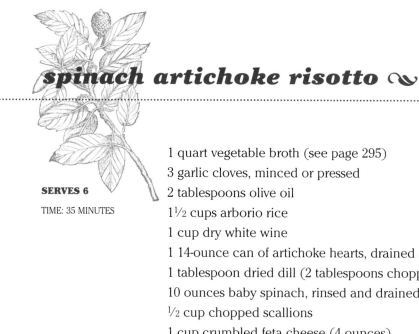

SERVES 6

TIME: 35 MINUTES

1 quart vegetable broth (see page 295)
3 garlic cloves, minced or pressed
2 tablespoons olive oil
1½ cups arborio rice
1 cup dry white wine
1 14-ounce can of artichoke hearts, drained and quartered
1 tablespoon dried dill (2 tablespoons chopped fresh)
10 ounces baby spinach, rinsed and drained
½ cup chopped scallions
1 cup crumbled feta cheese (4 ounces)

In a saucepan, bring the broth to a boil and then reduce the heat to maintain a gentle simmer.

In a large, heavy saucepan on medium-high heat, cook the garlic in the oil until golden, just a few seconds. Add the rice, stirring to coat each grain with oil. Stir in the wine, artichoke hearts, and dill if using dried. Cook, stirring often, until the wine is absorbed. Ladle in the hot broth a cup at a time, stirring frequently. After each addition, cook until the rice has absorbed most of the broth before adding the next ladleful.

When most of the broth is absorbed and the rice is tender but still al dente, stir in the spinach, in batches if necessary. When the spinach is wilted but still bright green, remove the pan from the heat and stir in the scallions, feta cheese, and dill if using fresh. Serve at once.

serving & menu ideas ⌀

For a beautiful supper, serve Spinach Artichoke Risotto with Carrot Salad with Raspberry Vinaigrette (page 217) and have fresh strawberries for dessert.

spinach polenta topped with tomatoes ↶

This polenta, chock-full of earthy spinach, contrasts beautifully
in both flavor and color with the sweet-tart tomatoes.
(See photo on page 86.)

SERVES 4

TIME: 25 MINUTES

SPINACH POLENTA

2 cups water

2 cups milk

1 teaspoon salt

1 cup polenta cornmeal (see page 177)

1 cup grated Parmesan cheese

8 ounces fresh baby spinach

FRESH TOMATO TOPPING

4 large tomatoes or 8 to 10 plum tomatoes

2 garlic cloves, minced or pressed

2 tablespoons olive oil

$^1/_2$ teaspoon salt

1 teaspoon dried oregano

2 tablespoons balsamic vinegar

To make the polenta: In a saucepan, bring the water, milk, and salt to a boil. Add the cornmeal in a slow, steady stream while whisking. Simmer for about 5 minutes, stirring occasionally, until the polenta is thick.

Meanwhile, prepare the topping: Cut the tomatoes into wedges. In a saucepan on medium-low heat, cook the garlic in the oil for a minute. Add the tomatoes, salt, oregano, and vinegar and simmer for about 5 minutes, just until hot.

When the polenta is thick, reduce the heat to low and stir in the cheese until melted and smooth. Fold in the spinach, a couple of handfuls at a time, until just wilted.

Serve the polenta hot, topped with the tomatoes and more cheese if you wish.

mexican polenta-stuffed peppers ~

5 large bell peppers (green, red, yellow, orange, or a combination)
1½ tablespoons olive oil
sprinkling of salt

SERVES 4 TO 6

TIME: 45 MINUTES

POLENTA

4 cups water
½ teaspoon salt
¼ teaspoon red pepper flakes (optional)
1 cup polenta cornmeal (see page 177)
1½ cups corn kernels
1 tablespoon olive oil or butter
1½ cups grated sharp Cheddar cheese
½ cup chopped Spanish olives

SALSA

1 16-ounce jar of your favorite salsa
1 15-ounce can of black beans, drained
¼ cup chopped cilantro (optional)

Preheat the oven to 450°. Cut the peppers in half lengthwise and remove the seeds, but leave the stem ends on so the peppers will hold their shape. Brush the pepper halves with oil, inside and out, and sprinkle lightly with salt. Place cut-side up on an oiled baking sheet and roast in the oven until tender but still holding their shape, about 15 minutes.

While the peppers roast, in a heavy saucepan, bring the water, salt, and red pepper flakes to a boil. Add the polenta in a slow, steady stream while whisking. Cook on medium heat, stirring often, until thickened. Stir in the corn, oil or butter, 1 cup of the cheese, and the olives. Remove from the heat.

Fill the roasted pepper halves with the polenta mixture. Sprinkle the tops with the remaining cheese and return to the oven for 5 to 10 minutes, until the cheese is melted. Meanwhile, combine the salsa, black beans, and cilantro in a saucepan and bring to a simmer.

To serve, spoon some of the black bean salsa on each dinner plate and place one or two pepper halves on top.

serving & menu ideas ☙

This is a complete, filling dinner that needs no accompaniment, although a green salad with Caesar Dressing (page 220) is always nice. For that matter, Peanut Butter Chocolate Sauce (page 280) on vanilla ice cream is always nice, too.

green fried rice ∾

Any rice is fine for this dish, but Lemongrass Rice (page 181) makes it particularly flavorful. We especially like this technique for cooking eggs for fried rice.

SERVES 4

TIME: 30 MINUTES

3 tablespoons vegetable oil

1 teaspoon Chinese chili paste (optional)

1 teaspoon salt

2 garlic cloves, minced

4 eggs, beaten

4 or 5 stalks bok choy, chopped into bite-sized pieces (about 4 cups)

1 bunch scallions, chopped

4 cups rinsed and drained baby spinach (3 or 4 ounces)

1 cup fresh or frozen corn kernels

2 cups cooked rice

1 tablespoon soy sauce

Before you begin to stir-fry, have everything prepped and close at hand: Cook rice if you don't have leftovers, chop the vegetables, and beat the eggs.

In a large wok (or you could use a skillet) on medium-high heat, warm half of the oil, chili paste, salt, and garlic. Sizzle for a few seconds, mashing the chili paste into the oil. Pour the eggs into the hot oil and cook, scraping the cooked egg toward the center and tilting the pan so the liquid egg spreads and cooks. Cut into bite-sized pieces and transfer to a bowl.

Wipe out the pan and heat the remaining oil, chili paste, salt, and garlic. Add the bok choy and stir-fry for a minute. Add the scallions and spinach and stir-fry until the spinach is just wilted. Add the corn and stir-fry for another minute. Stir in the rice. When the rice is hot, mix in the soy sauce and the cooked eggs. Serve immediately.

serving & menu ideas ∾

Round out this simple Asian supper with Spicy Tofu (page 65) and a Pineapple Ginger Shake (page 281).

lemony couscous with chickpeas ❧

This elegant herbed couscous is a lemon lover's delight. We like it best made with all of the herbs. The flavor develops beautifully overnight in the refrigerator.

SERVES 4 TO 6

TIME: 20 MINUTES

1$\frac{1}{2}$ cups couscous

$\frac{1}{2}$ teaspoon salt

2$\frac{1}{2}$ cups boiling water

2 lemons

$\frac{1}{4}$ cup olive oil

1 14-ounce can of chickpeas, rinsed and drained

1 cup chopped black olives

ONE OR MORE:

❧ 2 tablespoons minced fresh dill

❧ $\frac{1}{2}$ cup finely chopped fresh parsley

❧ $\frac{1}{2}$ cup finely chopped scallions

❧ $\frac{1}{2}$ cup minced fresh mint

$\frac{1}{2}$ cup chopped toasted almonds

Put the couscous and salt in a bowl and pour the boiling water over it. Cover and set aside for about 10 minutes, until the water is absorbed. Grate the lemon peels (see page 290) and juice the lemons. Stir together the lemon zest, $\frac{1}{4}$ cup of juice, and the olive oil.

Fluff the couscous with a fork, separating any lumps. Add the chickpeas, olives, the lemon and oil mixture, and the herbs and toss well. Add more salt to taste. Serve at room temperature or chilled. Top with the toasted almonds just before serving.

INGREDIENT NOTE Instead of fresh mint, add about a tablespoon of herbal spearmint or peppermint tea (1 teabag) when you add the water to the dry couscous.

serving & menu ideas ❧

We like Peppercorn Citrus Marinated Feta (page 201) on this salad and steamed artichokes with Gremolata Butter (page 237) or Herbed Aioli (page 224) on the side.

quinoa & vegetable pilaf ∾

Quinoa is an ancient high-protein grain from Peru that has made its way into North American cooking. Here we combine it with vegetables and herbs for a quick and well-rounded meal. Cooking quinoa in broth makes a big difference in flavor.

SERVES 4

TIME: 30 MINUTES

1½ cups raw quinoa
2¼ cups vegetable broth (see page 295)
1 teaspoon dried thyme
1 onion, diced
2 garlic cloves, minced or pressed
1 tablespoon olive oil
2 carrots, peeled and diced
1 bell pepper, seeded and diced
1 cup fresh or frozen green peas
1 tomato, diced
½ teaspoon salt
¼ teaspoon black pepper
grated Parmesan, Cheddar, or feta cheese (optional)

Thoroughly rinse and drain the quinoa in a fine mesh strainer (rinsing removes the residue of the grain's bitter coating). In a covered saucepan on high heat, bring the quinoa, broth, and thyme to a boil. Reduce the heat to low and simmer covered until all the liquid is absorbed, 15 to 20 minutes. Fluff with a fork. Cover and set aside.

While the quinoa cooks, sauté the onion and garlic in the oil in a skillet on medium-high heat for 3 or 4 minutes, until softened. Add the carrots and sauté for 3 or 4 minutes, stirring occasionally and covering the skillet, if necessary, to prevent sticking. Add the bell pepper and peas and sauté just until they are hot, a couple of minutes. Stir in the tomato, salt, and pepper, cover, and remove from the heat.

When both the quinoa and vegetables are done, combine them. Add salt to taste. Serve topped with cheese if you wish.

INGREDIENT NOTES Use different vegetables, such as asparagus, green beans, celery, and mushrooms—just be sure there are several colors and about 4 to 5 cups total.

Vary the herb—try dill, tarragon, or rosemary.

serving & menu ideas ∾

Serve with Lemon Herb Tofu (page 68), corn on the cob with one of our toppings (page 188), or Broccoli Tomato Salad (page 204).

kasha & orzo with portabellas ～

We were happy to discover that orzo and kasha can be cooked together. When we added the rich flavor and texture of portabellas and walnuts, we knew we had a winner.

SERVES 4

TIME: 35 MINUTES

3 cups chopped onions

2 large portabella mushrooms or 10 ounces cremini
   mushrooms, chopped

2 tablespoons olive oil

2 garlic cloves, minced or pressed

$\frac{1}{2}$ teaspoon dried thyme (2 teaspoons chopped fresh)

$\frac{1}{2}$ teaspoon salt

1 egg

$\frac{1}{2}$ cup kasha (see page 177)

$\frac{1}{2}$ cup orzo

2 cups boiling water

2 tablespoons butter

salt and pepper

sour cream

toasted walnuts

In a large saucepan or skillet on medium-high heat, cook the onions and mushrooms in the oil with the garlic, thyme, and salt until the onions are translucent, about 8 minutes.

In a bowl, lightly beat the egg. Add the kasha, stir to coat well, and add to the skillet and cook, stirring constantly, until the egg is dry, making sure to separate any clumps of kasha. Add the orzo and the boiling water, cover, reduce the heat to low, and simmer for about 15 minutes.

When the kasha and orzo are tender, stir in the butter. Add salt and pepper to taste. Serve topped with sour cream and toasted walnuts.

variations ∾

Add a chopped red bell pepper to the onions and mushrooms after they've been cooking for about 5 minutes.

Almost any sautéed chopped vegetable can be incorporated into this dish—try whatever appeals to you or what you find in your refrigerator waiting to be used up. Maybe carrots or zucchini, green peas, a leafy green, or even asparagus.

For a richer flavor, use half water and half vegetable broth. Omit the salt if the broth is salted.

serving & menu ideas ∾

This warm, comforting dish cries out for a light, tangy accompaniment. We like it with Corn & Pepper Salad (page 207) or Beet Salad (page 209). For dessert, consider Apples Two Ways (page 191), Cherry Shortbread Crumble (page 265), or Riesling Roasted Pears (page 264).

Warm French Lentil Salad (page 112)

main dish salads

southwestern black bean salad ∾

A beautiful-looking meal with a multitude of colors, flavors, and textures just right for hot weather and as a festive cold-weather treat as well.

SERVES 4

TIME: 15 MINUTES

1 15-ounce can of black beans, rinsed and drained
1½ cups cooked corn kernels
½ cup Cilantro Lime Dressing (page 225)
2 avocados
8 cups salad greens
tortilla chips
chopped green olives (optional)
sour cream or grated cheese (optional)

In a bowl, toss the beans and corn with the Cilantro Lime Dressing. Peel and pit the avocados and cut them into wedges or cubes.

Arrange the salad greens on individual serving plates and mound the bean and corn salad in the center. Top with the avocado wedges and ring the bean salad with tortilla chips. If you wish, top with olives and sour cream or grated cheese.

serving & menu ideas ∾

For a regional theme, start with Southwestern Cheese Soup (see page 129).

potato salad with green & white beans ⌀

Make a double batch because you're sure to want leftovers—this makes a great lunch the next day.

SERVES 4 TO 6

TIME: 30 MINUTES

5 red potatoes (about 1½ pounds)
1 pound green beans
½ cup olive oil
3 tablespoons cider vinegar
½ teaspoon salt
¼ teaspoon black pepper
2 tablespoons chopped fresh basil
⅓ cup thinly sliced red onions
1 15-ounce can of white beans, rinsed and drained

Bring a large pot of salted water to a boil. Meanwhile, cut each potato in half and then into ½ inch-thick slices. Add the potatoes to the boiling water and cook until just tender, about 10 minutes.

While the potatoes are cooking, cut the stem ends off the green beans and snap them in half. In a large serving bowl, whisk together the oil, vinegar, salt, and pepper. Stir in the basil and onions.

When the potatoes are done, lift them out of the water with a large slotted spoon or a mesh strainer and place them in the serving bowl. Return the water to a boil. Add the green beans and cook until crisp-tender, about 5 minutes.

Drain the green beans and add them to the bowl. Add the white beans and gently toss everything together. Add more salt and pepper to taste. This salad is delicious warm, at room temperature, or chilled.

serving & menu ideas ⌀

Serve with cheese and bread, or with sliced tomatoes and corn on the cob with one of our delicious toppings (page 188). Turn leftovers into a Niçoise salad by adding olives and hard-boiled eggs or tuna.

indian potato salad with cilantro omelet ✎

The potato salad is delicious on its own, and so is the omelet.
Together? Divine.

INDIAN POTATO SALAD

SERVES 4

TIME: 40 MINUTES

4 cups cubed potatoes (1-inch cubes)

3 tablespoons vegetable oil

2 teaspoons whole cumin seeds

$1^{1}/_{2}$ teaspoons salt

$1^{1}/_{2}$ teaspoons Curry Powder (page 238) or garam masala

pinch of cayenne or a splash of Tabasco or other hot pepper sauce

2 or 3 scallions, sliced

1 red bell pepper, chopped

$^{1}/_{4}$ cup chopped fresh cilantro

CILANTRO OMELET

4 eggs

1 tablespoon vegetable oil

$^{1}/_{4}$ cup chopped fresh cilantro

salt

plain yogurt

To cook the potatoes, bring a pot of salted water to a boil. Lower the potatoes into the hot water and cook until tender but not falling apart, about 5 minutes after the water returns to a boil. While the potatoes cook, warm the oil in a saucepan on medium heat. Sizzle the cumin seeds for a few seconds and then stir in the salt, curry powder, and cayenne. Remove from the heat. Drain the cooked potatoes and place them in a bowl. Pour the hot seasoned oil over the potatoes and add the scallions, bell pepper, and cilantro. Stir gently and set aside.

To make the omelet, whisk the eggs in a small bowl until frothy. Heat the oil in a skillet on medium heat. Pour the eggs into the skillet. When the bottom is set, sprinkle on the cilantro and a little salt and fold the omelet in half. Cook covered until the eggs are set and the bottom is browned. Slice into wedges.

Serve each wedge of warm omelet with potato salad topped with a dollop of yogurt.

INGREDIENT NOTES Replace the salt with 1½ teaspoons Cumin Salt (page 241) and keep or omit the cumin seeds.

In this potato salad, we love the flavor of our homemade Curry Powder.

serving & menu ideas ◌

This is a satisfying meal as is, but if you want to indulge, serve one of our chutneys on the side (pages 229, 231). Have a cup of Red Lentil Soup with Greens (page 121) to start, and for dessert, Mango Coconut Sorbet (page 271) or Lemon Coconut Tapioca Pudding (page 276).

summer panzanella ~

This bread salad makes a perfect summer meal with its ripe juicy tomatoes, basil, olives, and fresh mozzarella all tossed with crusty bread to soak up every drop of the juice!

SERVES 4

TIME: 20 MINUTES

SITTING TIME:
AT LEAST 10 MINUTES

½ loaf of crusty French or Italian bread (about 8 ounces)
4 tomatoes
1 large ball of fresh mozzarella (about 5 ounces)
½ red onion
½ cup fresh basil leaves
1 cup pitted olives
1 tablespoon red wine vinegar or cider vinegar
1 tablespoon olive oil
salt and pepper
Versatile Vinaigrette (page 222) (optional)

Preheat the oven to 350°. Cut the bread in half lengthwise and place in the oven until crisp, 5 to 10 minutes.

Meanwhile, prepare the other ingredients and place them in a serving bowl: Cut the tomatoes and fresh mozzarella into ½-inch cubes (about 4 cups of tomatoes and 1 cup of mozzarella), peel and thinly slice the red onion, cut the basil leaves into thin strips, and chop the olives. Add the vinegar and oil to the bowl and toss well.

Cut the toasted bread into 1-inch cubes (7 to 8 cups). Add the bread cubes to the bowl and toss well. Let the salad sit for at least 10 minutes before serving, to allow the bread to soak up some of the juices. Add salt and pepper to taste. Pass vinaigrette at the table if you like.

serving & menu ideas ~

Think summer and make some summery sides, such as Lemony Green Beans (page 192) and Corn on the Cob (page 188) with Gremolata Butter (page 237).

caesar salad with tofu croutons ❧

Perfect for a luncheon or light supper, this nutritious salad combines the satisfying crunch of romaine lettuce with savory bites of tofu. (See photo on page 218.)

SERVES 4

TIME: 30 MINUTES

TOFU CROUTONS

1 cake firm tofu (about 16 ounces)
1 tablespoon olive oil
2 tablespoons soy sauce
1½ teaspoons rubbed sage
1 tablespoon ground fennel seeds
¼ teaspoon red pepper flakes
3 garlic cloves, pressed or minced

1 head of romaine lettuce (about 8 cups sliced or torn leaves)
Caesar Dressing (page 220)
grated Parmesan or Pecorino Romano cheese (optional)

To make the Tofu Croutons, preheat the oven to 450°. Cut the tofu into 1-inch cubes and place them in a single layer in an oiled baking dish. In a small bowl, mix the oil, soy sauce, sage, fennel, red pepper, and garlic. Pour this marinade over the tofu and stir well. Bake until the edges of the tofu are crisp and most of the liquid has evaporated, about 25 minutes. Stir the tofu once or twice during baking.

Meanwhile, rinse and dry the lettuce leaves. Slice or tear them into bite-sized pieces and place in a large salad bowl. Prepare the Caesar Dressing.

Just before serving, toss the lettuce with some of the dressing. Pass the Tofu Croutons, grated cheese, and more dressing at the table.

serving & menu ideas ❧

Serve with a crusty baguette and sweet butter. On a night when a soup and salad supper would hit the spot, heat up some Creamy Onion Soup with Sherry (page 132).

vietnamese noodle salad ∾

For a richer dressing, add half a cup of coconut milk and a couple of tablespoons of peanut butter to the dressing.

SERVES 4

TIME: 25 MINUTES

8 ounces wide rice noodles

DRESSING
¼ cup lime juice
¼ cup vegetable oil
2 tablespoons dark sesame oil
1 teaspoon Chinese chili paste, or to taste
¼ cup chopped fresh basil and/or cilantro
½ teaspoon salt

1 cucumber
1 carrot
4 scallions
4 ounces seasoned tofu
toasted peanuts

Bring a large covered pot of salted water to a boil. Add the noodles and cook until tender, about 5 minutes. Drain the noodles, rinse with cold water, and drain again.

Meanwhile, in a large bowl, whisk together all of the dressing ingredients. (For a smoother dressing, purée in a blender.) Prepare the vegetables and tofu and add them to the bowl with the dressing: Peel, halve, and seed the cucumber, and then cut the halves into ¼ inch-thick crescents. Peel the carrot and cut it into matchsticks. Slice the scallions on the diagonal. Cut the tofu into matchsticks. Add the noodles to the bowl and toss well. Serve at room temperature, sprinkled with peanuts.

serving & menu ideas ∾

Change the menu with the seasons: Serve with cool, crunchy Pan-Asian Slaw (page 212) in the summer and with savory Indonesian Sweet Potato & Cabbage Soup (page 122) when it's cold outside.

warm french lentil salad ∿

....

*The warmth of this salad brings out the best flavors of the
ingredients: mellow lentils, sharp escarole, aromatic fennel,
and rich, crunchy walnuts. (See photo on page 102.)*

SERVES 4

TIME: 40 MINUTES

1 cup French lentils

1 teaspoon salt

1 medium head of escarole (about 12 ounces)

1 fresh fennel bulb

2 tablespoons olive oil or walnut oil

3 garlic cloves, minced or pressed

2 teaspoons ground fennel seeds

1½ teaspoons dried thyme (1 to 2 tablespoons chopped fresh)

¾ cup chopped toasted walnuts

lemon wedges or a cruet of vinegar

In a saucepan, bring the lentils, 3 cups of water, and ½ teaspoon of the salt to a simmer. Cover and cook for about 30 minutes, until the lentils are tender but not mushy.

Meanwhile, rinse, drain, and chop the escarole (about 6 cups). To prepare the fennel bulb, remove the outer layers if bruised or soft. Cut in half lengthwise, remove the hard core, and thinly slice (about 2 cups).

In a large skillet, heat the oil and sauté the garlic, ground fennel, and thyme for a few seconds. Add the fresh fennel and the remaining ½ teaspoon salt and stir-fry on high heat for about 2 minutes. Stir in the escarole and cook for another 2 minutes or so, until softened but still crisp and bright. Remove from the heat and drain any excess liquid into the cooking lentils.

When the lentils are done, drain them. Stir the drained lentils into the escarole mixture. Serve the salad warm or at room temperature, topped with the walnuts. Decorate with lemon wedges, or offer vinegar at the table.

INGREDIENT NOTE French lentils (also called du Puy lentils) are small and dark. They cook quickly and hold their shape nicely. Look for French lentils where other lentils are sold in your market.

variation ∽

In place of fresh fennel, use 1$\frac{1}{2}$ cups thinly sliced celery.

serving & menu ideas ∽

Decorate French Lentil Salad with tomato wedges and chèvre or feta. Serve with Asparagus Avgolemono (page 130) and crusty French or Italian bread with good olive oil for dipping.

Mushroom Miso Soup (page 128)

soups

mushroom tortellini soup ∿

With tortellini in the freezer and dried mushrooms and a carton of broth in your pantry, you can throw together this savory, filling soup in only half an hour.

SERVES 4

YIELDS 6 CUPS

TIME: 30 MINUTES

$\frac{1}{2}$ ounce dried porcini or portabella mushrooms

2 cups boiling water

2 cups diced onions

1 tablespoon olive oil or butter

1 teaspoon dried thyme

1 quart mushroom broth (see page 295)

1 9-ounce package of fresh or frozen tortellini (cheese, mushroom, or sun-dried tomato filled)

salt and pepper

sour cream or grated Parmesan cheese (optional)

Place the dried mushrooms in a heatproof bowl and pour the boiling water over them. Set aside until the mushrooms soften, about 15 minutes.

While the dried mushrooms are soaking, in a soup pot on medium-high heat, cook the onions in the olive oil, stirring frequently, until softened, 8 to 10 minutes. Stir in the thyme and add the broth. Remove the mushrooms from the soaking liquid, rinse if needed to remove grit, chop, and add to the soup. Pour the soaking liquid through a coffee filter or paper towel if it is gritty and add it to the soup. Bring to a boil.

Add the tortellini to the boiling soup and cook until al dente: for fresh tortellini, 3 to 4 minutes; for frozen tortellini, 8 to 9 minutes. Add salt and pepper to taste. Serve hot, topped with sour cream or grated cheese if you like.

serving & menu ideas ∿

Start with Caesar Salad with Tofu Croutons (page 109) or with crudités and Herbed Hummus (page 253) or Bean & Walnut Spread (page 255). Finish with one of the Fruit & Cheese Plates (page 260)—try plums or pears with Manchego cheese.

tomato tortilla soup ∾

This thick, flavorful Southwestern soup comes together easily using pantry items.

SERVES 4 TO 6

YIELDS 9 CUPS

TIME: 35 MINUTES

3 cups diced onions

2 teaspoons olive oil

2 teaspoons ground cumin

1 teaspoon dried oregano

1 quart vegetable broth (see page 295)

1 28-ounce can of diced tomatoes

2 teaspoons minced canned chipotles in adobo sauce
(see page 286), or more to taste

1½ cups crumbled corn tortilla chips

In a soup pot on medium heat, cook the onions in the oil for 5 minutes or until softened. Add the cumin and oregano and stir for a minute. Add the broth, tomatoes, and chipotles, cover, and bring to a boil. Reduce the heat and simmer for about 10 minutes.

Pulverize the tortilla chips in a blender. Add about 3 cups of the hot soup to the blender and purée until smooth. To make pouring easier, add another cup of hot soup and whirl on low speed. Stir the purée into the simmering soup pot. Serve hot.

serving & menu ideas ∾

Garnish the soup with chopped avocados, sour cream, grated cheese, and/or chopped fresh cilantro. For a complete Mexican-style supper, pair the soup with Bean & Cheese Quesadillas (page 141). Assemble the quesadillas while the soup cooks. Serve natural lime frozen fruit bars or Mango Coconut Sorbet (page 271) for dessert.

thai butternut squash soup ∽

....

This creamy vegan soup is spicy and a little sweet.

SERVES 4

YIELDS 7 CUPS

TIME: 30 MINUTES

1 cup coconut milk

½ teaspoon Thai red curry paste

4 teaspoons sugar

½ teaspoon salt

2 cups vegetable broth (see page 295)

1 Keiffer lime leaf (optional)

2 12-ounce packages of frozen cooked winter squash

1 lime

2 cups fresh baby spinach

chopped fresh cilantro (optional)

PAN-FRIED TOFU

½ cake firm tofu (about 8 ounces)

1 tablespoon soy sauce

½ teaspoon Thai red curry paste

1 teaspoon vegetable oil

In a soup pot, whisk together the coconut milk, curry paste, sugar, salt, and broth. Add the lime leaf and frozen squash, cover, and bring to a simmer. Cook, covered, until the squash is thawed, about 15 minutes.

Meanwhile, prepare the Pan-Fried Tofu. Cut the tofu into small cubes and put them in a bowl. Toss with the soy sauce and the curry paste. Heat the oil in a small skillet on medium-high heat. When the oil is hot, add the tofu and cook, stirring occasionally, for about 5 minutes. Set aside.

Lightly grate the lime peel and juice the lime. Add 1 teaspoon of the zest and 2 table-spoons of the juice to the simmering soup. Stir in the spinach and tofu and cook just until the spinach wilts. Add more sugar and salt to taste. Serve the soup garnished with cilantro if you like.

INGREDIENT NOTES We like Thai Kitchen brand red curry paste, found in the Asian section of well-stocked supermarkets.

Packaged frozen winter squash is perfect for this recipe, but if it's not available, look for pre-cut butternut squash in the produce section of your market, or peel and seed your own squash. You'll need 4 cups chopped. Purée the soup in a blender before adding the spinach and tofu.

variation ∾

Substitute ½ pound of peeled and deveined shrimp for the tofu. You can either pan-fry them as you would the tofu, or cook them for 4 or 5 minutes in the simmering soup before adding the spinach.

curried cauliflower & chickpea soup ∾

This soup was inspired by the cauliflower curry we regularly make at Moosewood Restaurant. The chutney makes it perfect. (See photo on page 230.)

SERVES 4 TO 6

YIELDS 8 CUPS

TIME: 35 MINUTES

1½ cups chopped onions

1 tablespoon vegetable oil

1½ tablespoons grated peeled ginger root

1½ tablespoons curry powder

½ teaspoon salt

1 15-ounce can of chickpeas, drained

3 cups water or vegetable broth (see page 295)

1 small head of cauliflower

1 28-ounce can of diced tomatoes

Cranberry Chutney (page 231), Pineapple Chutney (page 229), or your favorite prepared chutney

a few sprigs of cilantro (optional)

In a soup pot on medium heat, cook the onions in the oil for a few minutes, until they begin to soften. Add the ginger, curry powder, and salt and sauté for a minute or two, stirring constantly so the spices don't burn. Add the chickpeas and the water, cover, and bring to a boil.

Meanwhile, cut the cauliflower into bite-sized pieces (about 4 cups). When the water boils, stir in the cauliflower and tomatoes, reduce the heat, cover, and simmer until the cauliflower is tender, about 5 minutes.

When the cauliflower is done, remove the pot from the heat. Purée 2 or 3 cups of the soup in a blender and stir it back into the pot. Top each bowl of soup with a large spoonful of chutney and a sprig of cilantro.

serving & menu ideas ∾

Serve warm chapatis or naan bread with this spicy soup.

red lentil soup with greens ∾

This ginger- and licorice-flavored soup chock-full of greens is a gratifying supper any time of year.

SERVES 4

YIELDS 6 CUPS

TIME: 30 MINUTES

1¼ cups red lentils

1 teaspoon salt

2 tablespoons vegetable oil

1½ teaspoons black mustard seeds (optional)

1½ teaspoons anise or fennel seeds

¼ to ½ teaspoon red pepper flakes

1 teaspoon ground ginger, or 2 tablespoons grated
    peeled ginger root

1 garlic clove, pressed or minced

4 cups rinsed, drained, and chopped fresh mustard greens,
    Swiss chard, or spinach

½ teaspoon salt

¾ cup coconut milk

Rinse the lentils and drain. In a soup pot, bring 5 cups of water, the lentils, and salt to a boil. Reduce the heat to a simmer, cover, and cook until tender, about 30 minutes.

While the lentils cook, warm the oil in a saucepan on medium heat, add the black mustard seeds, and cover until they pop. Stir in the anise, red pepper flakes, ginger, and garlic and cook for a minute, stirring constantly. Add the greens and the salt and cook, stirring frequently, until the greens are just wilted. Stir in the coconut milk and simmer for a minute. Remove from the heat.

When the lentils are soft, stir in the greens and coconut milk mixture and add salt to taste.

serving & menu ideas ∾

A Greek Salad (page 211) or baby greens dressed with Caesar Dressing (page 220) would be welcome beside a bowl of this soup.

indonesian sweet potato & cabbage soup ∿

A hearty soup inspired by Indonesian gado gado *sauce, fragrant and spicy with ginger and cayenne, rich with peanut butter and sweet potatoes.*

SERVES 4

YIELDS 8 CUPS

TIME: 40 MINUTES

1 tablespoon grated peeled ginger root

2 garlic cloves, minced or pressed

¼ to ½ teaspoon cayenne, or to taste

1 tablespoon vegetable oil

1½ cups chopped onions

½ teaspoon salt

2½ cups chopped cabbage (½-inch pieces)

2½ cups diced sweet potatoes (about 1 pound)

1 quart vegetable broth (see page 295)

½ cup peanut butter

1 cup chopped tomatoes

1 tablespoon soy sauce

mung bean sprouts (optional)

chopped cilantro, scallions, mint, and/or Thai basil (optional)

In a soup pot on medium heat, cook the ginger, garlic, and cayenne in the oil for a minute before adding the onions and salt. Cover and cook, stirring often, until the onions soften, about 5 minutes.

Stir in the cabbage and sweet potatoes. Add about 3½ cups of the broth. Cover and increase the heat to bring to a boil. Then reduce the heat and simmer for 15 minutes.

In a bowl, whisk together the peanut butter and the remaining ½ cup of broth until smooth. Add the peanut butter mixture to the soup with the tomatoes and soy sauce. Simmer covered until all the vegetables are tender, about 5 minutes.

Serve each bowl topped with bean sprouts and cilantro, scallions, mint, and/or basil.

red bean, potato & arugula soup ❧

Wish you were in Tuscany? Have this soup for supper as a small consolation.

SERVES 4

YIELDS 7 CUPS

TIME: 30 MINUTES

2 cups chopped onions
2 garlic cloves, minced or pressed
2 tablespoons olive oil
3 cups diced red potatoes
1 sprig of fresh rosemary (about 4 inches long)
3 cups vegetable broth (see page 295)
1 teaspoon salt
1 14-ounce can of small red beans, drained
½ cup white wine, or 2 tablespoons lemon juice
4 ounces arugula (about 4 cups)
¼ cup chopped fresh basil
salt and black pepper
lemon wedges (optional)
grated Parmesan or Pecorino Romano cheese (optional)

In a soup pot, sauté the onions and garlic in the oil for about 2 minutes. Add the potatoes, rosemary, broth, and salt. Cover and bring to a boil. Add the beans and the wine. Reduce the heat and simmer, covered, until the potatoes are tender, about 10 minutes.

While the potatoes cook, rinse and drain the arugula. Remove any large or tough stems and coarsely chop any large leaves. Set aside.

When the potatoes are tender, add the basil and salt and pepper to taste. Remove and discard the rosemary sprig—some leaves may stay behind in the soup, and that's fine. Put a handful of arugula into each bowl and ladle the hot soup over it. Serve immediately with lemon wedges and/or cheese.

serving & menu ideas ❧

Start with salad greens with Sour Cream Lemon Dressing (page 223) and serve fresh fruit or Riesling Roasted Pears (page 264) for dessert.

beans, corn & greens soup ∾

This chunky soup is a satisfying supper in one bowl.

SERVES 4

YIELDS 7 CUPS

TIME: 25 TO 30 MINUTES

1 cup chopped onions

1 tablespoon olive oil

2 teaspoons ground cumin

1 teaspoon ground fennel

$\frac{1}{2}$ teaspoon red pepper flakes or $\frac{1}{4}$ teaspoon cayenne

2 cups rinsed, stemmed, and chopped kale or collards

salt

1 28-ounce can of diced tomatoes

1 15-ounce can of beans, drained (black, white, or red beans, field
  peas, black-eyed peas, etc.)

2 cups frozen corn kernels

1 cup water or vegetable broth (see page 295)

chopped fresh cilantro (optional)

In a pot on medium heat, sauté the onions in the oil until softened, 6 to 8 minutes. Stir in the cumin, fennel, red pepper, and kale. Sprinkle with salt, cover, and cook until the kale is wilted, 3 or 4 minutes. Add the tomatoes, beans, corn, and water and bring to a low boil, stirring often. Reduce the heat, cover, and simmer for about 10 minutes. Add more water for a brothier soup. Add salt to taste and stir in cilantro if you like.

INGREDIENT NOTES To prepare this soup in record time, skip chopping and cooking the onions and get flavor from salsa instead. (We like Herdez and Pace brands.) Instead of a 28-ounce can of diced tomatoes, use a 16-ounce jar of salsa and a 15-ounce can of diced tomatoes. And use frozen collards. Just heat everything but the greens in a soup pot. Add the collards when the soup is hot and simmer until they are tender.

serving & menu ideas ∾

Sometimes we like to top this soup with crumbled tortilla chips and/or grated cheese, such as Cheddar, Monterey Jack, or asadero.

italian bread & cheese soup ✺

This is the quintessential simple supper for many Italian families.

SERVES 4

TIME: 15 MINUTES

1 tablespoon olive oil
3 garlic cloves, minced or pressed (optional)
1 quart vegetable broth (see page 295)
4 ounces Fontina, Gruyère, or Cheddar cheese
4 slices whole wheat bread
¼ cup chopped fresh basil or parsley
black pepper

In a soup pot, warm the olive oil. Add the garlic and cook until just golden, not brown. Add the broth and bring to a simmer. Meanwhile, grate the cheese (about 2 cups).

When you're ready to serve the soup, toast the bread. Break each slice of toast into bite-sized pieces and place in individual soup bowls. Cover with about ½ cup of cheese. Sprinkle with basil or parsley and pepper. Ladle a cup of hot broth over the bread and cheese in each bowl and serve at once.

INGREDIENT NOTES We prefer whole wheat bread in this recipe because it has more flavor than white. Pumpernickel bread is another good option, great in combination with Cheddar cheese. And even though it gets soggy, toasting the bread makes a difference.

serving & menu ideas ✺

Put a handful of chopped tomatoes or spinach or arugula in the bottom of the bowl under the cheese. Or try leftover Fresh Tomato & Mozzarella Salad (page 213) on top of the bread in place of the cheese—scrumptious! Serve this soup with Broccoli Tomato Salad (page 204) or Tomatoes & Onions with Mint (page 205). Have crisp apples and toasted walnuts for dessert.

mushroom miso soup ∿

Broccoli and mushrooms make this miso soup a little bit unusual and a meal in itself. (See photo on page 114.)

SERVES 4

YIELDS 8 CUPS

TIME: 25 MINUTES

$\frac{1}{2}$ ounce of dried shiitake mushrooms (6 to 10 caps)

1 cup boiling water

1 tablespoon soy sauce

2 tablespoons mirin or 1 tablespoon sugar (optional)

8 ounces soft tofu

1 or 2 broccoli crowns

2 scallions

$\frac{1}{3}$ cup light miso, or more to taste

a few drops of dark sesame oil (optional)

Place the mushrooms in a small heatproof bowl and add the boiling water and the soy sauce and mirin or sugar. Cover and let sit until the mushrooms soften, about 15 minutes. While the mushrooms soak, bring $4\frac{1}{2}$ cups of water to a simmer in a pot. Meanwhile, cut the tofu into small cubes, cut the broccoli into small bite-sized pieces (about 2 cups), and slice the scallions on the diagonal.

When the mushrooms are soft, remove them from the soaking liquid. Pour the soaking liquid into the pot of water, being careful to leave any sediment behind in the bottom of the bowl. Remove and discard the mushroom stems and cut the caps into thin slices.

Put the miso into a small bowl. When the soup broth begins to simmer, ladle a little of the hot liquid into the miso to soften it, and set aside. Add the tofu, broccoli, and mushrooms to the simmering broth and cook for 2 to 3 minutes, until the broccoli is bright green and just tender. Remove the soup from the heat and stir in the miso. Serve immediately, topped with the scallions. If you like, add a drop or two of sesame oil to each bowl of soup.

variations ∿

The broccoli can be omitted or replaced with other vegetables, such as snow peas, shredded cabbage, or bok choy.

Add cooked rice or soba noodles to the soup just before serving.

southwestern cheese soup ∽

*Mildly spicy, really homey, and satisfying. We'd like to acknowl-
edge our friend Anne Kenney for the idea for this recipe.*

SERVES 4 TO 6

YIELDS 10 CUPS

TIME: 30 MINUTES

2 cups chopped onions

3 garlic cloves, minced or pressed

2 tablespoons olive oil

1 4.5-ounce can of chopped mild green chiles

3 cups diced potatoes

1 quart vegetable broth (see page 295)

1 15-ounce can of creamed corn

1 15-ounce can of diced tomatoes

2½ cups grated sharp Cheddar cheese

In a soup pot, sauté the onions and garlic in the oil until the onions are soft, about
10 minutes. Stir in the chiles and potatoes. Add the broth, cover, and bring to a boil. Add
the corn and tomatoes, cover, and simmer on low heat, stirring occasionally, until the
potatoes are tender, about 5 minutes.

Divide the cheese among four to six bowls. Ladle the hot soup over the cheese.

serving & menu ideas ∽

Serve with a green salad topped with avocado and jicama and dressed with Cilantro
Lime Dressing (page 225). A platter of refreshing watermelon and cantaloupe would be
perfect for dessert.

asparagus avgolemono ✎

*Try this variation of the familiar Greek egg-lemon soup
in the springtime when the first tender shoots of asparagus
hit the markets.*

SERVES 2 TO 4

YIELDS 5 CUPS

TIME: 25 MINUTES

1 quart vegetarian mock chicken or vegetable broth (see page 295)

¼ cup pastina, orzo, or similar small pasta

2 cups asparagus cut into 1½- to 1-inch lengths

1 tablespoon chopped fresh dill

2 eggs

2 tablespoons lemon juice

salt and pepper

In a soup pot, bring the broth to a boil. Add the pasta and cook until almost al dente, about 4 minutes for pastina and 8 minutes for orzo.

Add the asparagus and dill and simmer until the asparagus is just tender, about 5 minutes.

While the asparagus cooks, in a bowl, whisk the eggs and lemon juice. When the asparagus is tender, whisk a ladleful of the hot broth into the egg-lemon mixture. Lower the heat and slowly pour the egg mixture into the soup in a thin stream, stirring briskly all the while. Continue to stir until the soup is thickened somewhat and heated through, a couple of minutes. (Constant stirring and low heat prevent the eggs from curdling.) Add salt and pepper to taste.

variations ✎

Other green vegetables, such as chopped spinach, broccoli, and kale, may be substituted for the asparagus.

For a smooth soup, purée with an immersion blender or in batches in a blender.

serving & menu ideas ✎

Peppercorn Citrus Marinated Feta (page 201) with pita, Greek Salad (page 211), and Greek Antipasto Pita (page 149) all pair well with this soup.

creamy onion soup with sherry ෙ

Many of us think to eat creamed pearl onions only once or twice a year at holiday feasts. We thought it would be fun to turn the traditional side dish into a soup for any day of the week.

SERVES 4 TO 6

YIELDS 9 CUPS

TIME: 30 MINUTES

5 cups milk

2 tablespoons butter

1 16-ounce package of frozen pearl onions (whole small onions)

3 garlic cloves, pressed (optional)

1 teaspoon salt

¼ teaspoon black pepper

¼ teaspoon grated nutmeg, or more to taste

¼ cup unbleached white flour

¾ cup dry sherry

½ cup sour cream

CROUTONS

3 cups ½-inch cubes of crusty bread, such as sourdough, pumpernickel, rye, or French

2 tablespoons butter

1 tablespoon olive oil

¼ teaspoon dried thyme

¼ teaspoon dried marjoram

In a saucepan on medium heat, warm the milk and 1 cup of water to just under a simmer. Don't let the liquid boil. Cover and keep warm.

Meanwhile, in a soup pot, melt the butter. Stir in the onions, garlic, salt, pepper, and nutmeg. Cover and cook on low heat for 5 minutes, stirring occasionally.

Sprinkle the onions with the flour and stir for a minute. The butter and any liquid will be absorbed and the mixture will thicken. Stir in the sherry, cook for a couple of minutes, and then stir in the sour cream. Increase the heat to medium, add about 2 cups of the hot milk, and stir until smooth. Add the rest of the milk, lower the heat, and slowly bring to just below a simmer, stirring occasionally. Turn off the heat until the croutons are done.

To make the croutons, toast the bread cubes until crisp on the outside but still soft and moist on the inside. In a small pan on low heat, melt the butter. Add the olive oil, thyme, and marjoram and sizzle the herbs for a minute. Put the toasted bread cubes into a bowl, drizzle on the herbed butter, and toss well.

Serve the soup piping hot, topped with the croutons. A note of caution: Be careful when you bite into an onion! It may be surprisingly hot.

serving & menu ideas ∽
....

A side of Baby Greens with Pecans & Pears (page 206) or tangy Lemony Green Beans (page 192) complements this creamy soup. For dessert, try Apples Two Ways (page 191) or New England Squash Pie (page 277).

Greek Antipasto Pita (page 149)

sandwiches, wraps & rolls

crostini ∿

Crostini are toasted or grilled slices of bread with tasty toppings, often served as an appetizer. For a relaxed supper, put a plate of toasted baguette slices and bowls of various toppings on the table (however many you like or have time to make) and have a make-your-own crostini simple supper night.

THE BREAD:

Many bakeries can thinly slice a baguette for you in their slicing machine. You usually get about 25 slices per average baguette. Each of the toppings recipes makes enough topping for 15 to 20 baguette-sized crostini, although the number depends on how high you pile the toppings. Of course, you can make crostini with the larger Italian or French loaves, also. The slices should be ¼- to ½-inch thick.

Toast the baguette slices. There is a difference of opinion on how toasty they should be: Some people like them just lightly toasted, while others like them very dry and crisp, almost like croutons. The bread can be toasted a couple of hours or even days ahead of time. When the slices are cool, store them in a well-sealed container or plastic bag until you're ready to assemble the crostini.

blue cheese topping ∿

TIME: 5 MINUTES

3 ounces blue cheese
3 ounces cream cheese, at room temperature
2 tablespoons milk, or more if needed
toasted walnut halves

Crumble the blue cheese into a bowl and mash it a bit with a fork. Mix in the cream cheese, adding a little milk if necessary to get a spreadable consistency. Spread about 2 teaspoons of the blue cheese mixture on each baguette slice and top with a walnut.

watercress topping ⌒

TIME: 10 TO 15 MINUTES

2 bunches of watercress
   (about 6 cups chopped)
4 garlic cloves, chopped
1 tablespoon olive oil
salt and pepper

Rinse the watercress, holding it in loose bouquets. Coarsely chop: Starting at the top, cut through the bunch about every inch until only stems without leaves are left. Discard the stems.

In a skillet on medium-low heat, sauté the garlic in the oil until golden. Add the watercress and sauté until wilted and bright green. Add salt and pepper to taste. Serve warm or at room temperature, piled on toasted baguette slices.

bell peppers & onions topping ⌒

TIME: 25 MINUTES

1 onion
2 large red, yellow and/or orange bell
   peppers
1 tablespoon olive oil
salt and pepper
4 small balls of fresh mozzarella cheese
   (optional)

Thinly slice the onion. Halve and seed the peppers and cut them into very thin strips.

Heat the oil in a skillet on medium heat. Add the onions and cook, stirring often, until softened, 3 to 4 minutes. Add the peppers and cook, stirring occasionally, until softened, 8 to 10 minutes. Add salt and pepper to taste. Serve warm or at room temperature on the baguette slices and top with thinly sliced rounds of fresh mozzarella.

serving & menu ideas ⌒
....

Other perfect toppings for crostini include Classic Pesto (page 252), Sicilian Chickpea Spread (page 254), Herbed Hummus (page 253), and Fresh Tomato & Mozzarella Salad (page 213).

    If you want to serve crostini as an appetizer before a main dish, the combination possibilities are endless. Here are some of our favorites: Watercress Crostini before Fettuccine with Walnut Pesto (page 25), Blue Cheese Crostini before Warm French Lentil Salad (page 112), Bell Peppers & Onions Crostini with Mushroom Tortellini Soup (page 116).

broccolini cheddar melt ∾

SERVES 2

TIME: 20 MINUTES

1 bunch broccolini (10 to 12 stems) or 1 large broccoli crown
3 garlic cloves, minced or pressed
2 teaspoons olive oil
salt and pepper
2 slices whole wheat or multigrain bread
3 ounces Cheddar cheese
Dijon or yellow mustard

Rinse the broccolini and chop it into ½ inch-long pieces. In a skillet on medium-high heat, cook the broccolini and the garlic in the oil for 4 or 5 minutes, until the broccolini is bright green and just tender. Sprinkle with salt and pepper. Add about ¼ cup of water to the pan and steam the broccolini until the water has evaporated. Remove from the heat.

While the broccolini cooks, toast the bread. Grate the cheese or cut it into thin slices. Spread mustard on the toast and place on a broiler pan.

Top each piece of toast with cooked broccolini and then cheese. Broil until the cheese is melted and bubbling, 3 to 5 minutes. Serve hot, open-faced.

INGREDIENT NOTE Broccolini, a cross between broccoli and Chinese kale, was introduced in supermarket produce departments a few years ago. It is milder tasting and more tender than broccoli, and the stalks don't need to be peeled.

serving & menu idea ∾

For soup and sandwich night, have some Red Bean, Potato & Arugula Soup (page 124).

seitan pizza subs ✐

It's just a short time from getting out the ingredients to sinking your teeth into these crusty rolls with a warm, soft filling.

SERVES 4

TIME: 15 MINUTES

4 sub rolls

1 cup tomato sauce, marinara sauce, or Simple Tomato Sauce (page 251)

8 ounces pepperoni-style sliced seitan

½ cup sliced pitted black olives

8 ounces sliced mozzarella cheese

Slice the rolls in half lengthwise and place them open and cut-side up on a baking tray. Lightly toast under the broiler.

Spread tomato sauce on both halves of each toasted roll. On the bottom halves, lay seitan slices in an overlapping pattern. Sprinkle the top halves with sliced olives and then cover with cheese. Broil until the cheese is melted and the seitan is hot. Put the halves back together and serve while hot.

INGREDIENT NOTES In place of sub rolls, use a long loaf of French or Italian bread cut into 5-inch lengths.

Look for pepperoni-style seitan slices in the refrigerator section near the tofu in natural foods stores and many supermarkets.

variation ✐

Sometimes we make these subs with pan-fried slices of portabellas instead of seitan.

serving & menu ideas ✐

Serve Broccoli Slaw (page 208) on the side and Chocolate Malts (page 281) for dessert.

bean & cheese quesadillas ∾

In about 10 minutes, this simple supper is in the oven, and just when you're tempted by the aroma, it's ready.

SERVES 4

HANDS-ON TIME:
10 MINUTES

BAKING TIME:
10 TO 15 MINUTES

1 16-ounce can of refried beans
8 flour tortillas (8- to 10-inch)
1 cup of your favorite salsa
$2^1/_2$ cups grated Monterey Jack cheese (about 8 ounces)

Preheat the oven to 400°.

Arrange 4 tortillas at least an inch apart on a lightly oiled baking sheet. Spread refried beans evenly over each tortilla. Spoon a couple of tablespoons of salsa on top of the beans and sprinkle with cheese. Place the remaining tortillas on top and press gently. Bake until the cheese is melted and the quesadillas are warmed through, 10 to 15 minutes.

Cut each quesadilla into 6 wedges and serve while hot, with more salsa on the side.

INGREDIENT NOTES If you can't find refried beans that you like, use plain pinto beans or black beans and mash them with the salsa before spreading on the tortillas.

variations ∾

Any number of other ingredients dress up these simple quesadillas: sliced olives, corn, chopped scallions, chopped green chiles, small cubes of cream cheese. But don't pile it on *too* thick or the filling will ooze out when you cut the quesadillas into wedges—about $1/_2$ inch deep is the maximum.

If you prefer a stovetop method, warm a lightly oiled skillet on medium heat. Cook the quesadillas for 2 to 3 minutes on each side, until the cheese is melted.

serving & menu ideas ∾

For a weeknight Mexican fiesta, serve with Tomato Tortilla Soup (page 117) and have Mango Coconut Sorbet (page 271) for dessert.

vegetarian reuben ∾

These open-faced sandwiches are not very traditional, rather messy—and very satisfying.

SERVES 4

TIME: 20 MINUTES

¼ cup mayonnaise

1 tablespoon ketchup

2 teaspoons white or cider vinegar

pinch of salt

black pepper to taste

pinch of sugar

1 8-ounce package of coleslaw mix or 4 cups finely shredded cabbage

8 thin slices of rye or pumpernickel bread, toasted

4 tomatoes, thinly sliced

8 ounces thinly sliced Swiss cheese

In a bowl large enough to hold the coleslaw mix, stir together the mayonnaise, ketchup, vinegar, salt, pepper, and sugar. Add the coleslaw and toss well.

Assemble the open-faced sandwiches on a baking sheet if you are going to use your oven broiler, or on trays if you're going to broil in batches in a toaster oven. Arrange the slices of toast an inch apart. Place about ¼ cup of coleslaw on each slice and top with tomato slices and then cheese.

Broil the sandwiches until the cheese melts, 3 to 5 minutes. Serve open-faced.

variations ∾

Use well-drained sauerkraut instead of coleslaw.

Add sliced seasoned tofu or Easy Baked Tofu (page 64).

serving & menu ideas ∾

Serve our Vegetarian Reuben deli-style with kosher dill pickle spears, potato chips or onion rings, and a 5-Minute Milkshake (page 281) for dessert.

tortilla melt ᕲ

Up to a day before baking, Tortilla Melts can be assembled, wrapped in foil, and refrigerated. Bake in the foil for about 15 minutes and then remove the foil and bake for about 5 minutes more for the tortillas to crisp. Leftovers can be refrigerated for up to a week and reheat well.

SERVES 2 TO 4

TIME: 45 MINUTES

3 tablespoons olive oil, plus more for brushing
    on the tortillas
1 tablespoon balsamic vinegar
2 large portabella mushroom caps
1 small red onion
salt and black pepper
6 flour tortillas (about 8 inches in diameter)
3 tablespoons cream cheese, softened
3 tablespoons jarred pesto or Classic Pesto (page 252),
    or $\frac{1}{2}$ cup chopped fresh basil
1 large tomato, sliced
6 ounces sliced mozzarella, smoked mozzarella,
    provolone, or a combination

Preheat the oven to 450°. Lightly oil a baking sheet.

In a bowl, whisk together 3 tablespoons of olive oil and the vinegar. Slice the portabellas and red onion and add to the bowl. Stir well to coat evenly with marinade. Spread on the baking sheet and sprinkle with salt and pepper. Roast in the oven until the onions are softened and the mushrooms are juicy, about 10 minutes. Remove from the oven and set aside. Reduce the oven temperature to 350°.

To build the sandwiches, lightly brush one side of two tortillas with oil and place them oiled-side down on a clean baking sheet. Spread the top side of the tortillas with cream cheese. Pile roasted portabellas and onions on the cream cheese. Spread pesto on two more tortillas and lay them on top of the onions. Top the pesto-covered tortillas with tomato and cheese slices. Place the last two tortillas on the stacks and brush the tops with oil. Bake until the cheese is melted and the top and bottom tortillas are crisp, about 15 minutes.

Let the sandwiches cool for a minute or two before cutting into quarters.

serving & menu ideas ∾

Although this sandwich is filling enough on its own, Red Bean, Potato & Arugula Soup (page 124) would be a nice accompaniment. Vanilla ice cream with one of our Two Sweet Sauces (page 280) would be the perfect dessert.

spinach cheese burritos

These burritos, with their creamy spinach filling, are one of the dishes that always elicit customer requests for the recipe when we serve them in the restaurant.

SERVES 4 TO 6

HANDS-ON TIME:
25 MINUTES

BAKING TIME:
20 TO 25 MINUTES

FILLING

1 bunch scallions, chopped

3 garlic cloves, pressed or minced

1 tablespoon vegetable oil

10 cups loosely packed fresh baby spinach (about 10 ounces)

1 teaspoon ground coriander

generous pinch of nutmeg (optional)

3 cups lightly packed grated Cheddar or Monterey Jack cheese
(about 10 ounces)

$1/3$ cup cream cheese (3 ounces)

8 to 10 flour tortillas (7- or 8-inch)

Blender Tomato Hot Sauce (page 244) or your favorite salsa

Preheat the oven to 375°. Oil a 9 x 13-inch baking dish.

In a large skillet on medium heat, cook the scallions and garlic in the oil for 2 or 3 minutes. Add the spinach and cook until the leaves are wilted and the water has evaporated. Stir in the coriander, nutmeg, cheese, and cream cheese. Remove from the heat.

To soften the tortillas so they won't crack when you roll them, lay out the tortillas on a baking sheet (overlapping is fine) and place in the oven for a minute or two.

To prepare the burritos, place about $1/2$ cup of filling on the lower half of a warm tortilla, fold the bottom up and the sides in to encase the filling, roll it up, and place seam-side down in the prepared baking dish. Repeat with the rest of the filling and tortillas. Brush the tops lightly with oil, cover the dish with foil, and bake until hot, 20 to 25 minutes. Serve topped with Blender Tomato Hot Sauce or salsa.

INGREDIENT NOTES If you want to use frozen spinach instead of fresh, look for bags with loose clumps of spinach instead of a solid block, and defrost before adding to the filling.

You can use thinly sliced onions instead of scallions.

serving & menu ideas ∾

We usually serve burritos on Yellow Rice (page 179) or plain brown or white rice. A crisp salad or a crunchy slaw is nice on the side. New England Squash Pie (page 277) would make the evening divine.

easy egg rolls ∾

These egg rolls made with filo dough bake in the oven, so there's no deep-frying. Crisp and delicious, they are a fine supper. They can be assembled a day ahead, wrapped in plastic, and refrigerated until they go into the oven.

SERVES 3

HANDS-ON TIME:
20 MINUTES

BAKING TIME:
20 MINUTES

1 tablespoon vegetable oil

1 tablespoon grated peeled ginger root

2 garlic cloves, minced or pressed

1 16-ounce package of slaw mix (about 6 cups) (see page 293)

1 tablespoon soy sauce

$\frac{1}{2}$ teaspoon salt

generous pinch of black pepper

6 sheets of filo pastry

about $\frac{1}{4}$ cup vegetable oil

Duck Sauce (page 228)

Preheat the oven to 375°. Lightly oil a baking sheet.

Warm a wok or large skillet on medium-high heat. Add the oil and when it is hot, add the ginger and garlic and sizzle for just a few seconds. Add the slaw, soy sauce, salt, and pepper and stir-fry for 3 or 4 minutes, until the vegetables are hot, coated with oil, and somewhat wilted but not soft. Remove from the heat.

Place the stack of filo sheets on a dry surface with the short sides at the top and bottom. Brush the top sheet lightly with oil. About 3 inches from the bottom edge, spread a generous cup of the wilted slaw in a line parallel to the bottom. Pick up 2 sheets at the bottom edge and lift them up and over the filling and roll up. Filo is fragile but forgiving; don't fret over small rips at the start. Brush the finished roll with oil. Lift it carefully and place on the prepared baking sheet. Repeat this process to make 2 more rolls. Place the rolls about 2 inches apart on the baking sheet. With a sharp knife, slice the rolls into 4-inch pieces. Bake until golden brown, about 20 minutes.

While the egg rolls bake, make the Duck Sauce to serve on the side.

greek antipasto pita ∾

This sandwich has been a favorite of Moosewood Restaurant's customers for more than 30 years. (See photo on page 134.)

SERVES 4 TO 6

TIME: 20 MINUTES

2 tablespoons olive oil

1 tablespoon red wine vinegar or cider vinegar

2 garlic cloves, minced or pressed

1 tablespoon chopped fresh dill

   (or 1 teaspoon dried dill or oregano)

1 celery stalk

1 large tomato

1/2 red bell pepper

1 cucumber

1/4 red onion

8 pitted kalamata olives

salt and pepper

4 pita breads

In a bowl, whisk together the oil, vinegar, garlic, and dill. As you prepare the vegetables, add them to the bowl: dice the celery, tomato, and bell pepper, seed and dice the cucumber, mince the red onion, chop the olives. Toss well. Add salt and pepper to taste. The filling tastes best if it sits at room temperature for at least 10 minutes. It will keep in the refrigerator for a couple of days.

Cut the pitas in half and toast them lightly. To serve, stuff each pita half with filling.

variation ∾

Add about 3 ounces of seasoned seitan, chopped. Look for seasoned seitan in the refrigerator section near the tofu in natural foods stores and many supermarkets.

serving & menu ideas ∾

Top with crumbled feta, diced fresh mozzarella, or shredded provolone cheese.

Shrimp Curry with Snow Peas (page 165)

fish

selecting & cooking fish

Seafood is a perfect ingredient for quickly prepared simple suppers—and there's no shortage of possibilities for variety. Some of the most easily prepared suppers for non-vegetarians are built around fish that is lightly seasoned or topped with a basic sauce. Steam, broil, bake, grill, pan-fry, or poach the fish—whichever procedure you prefer—and then top it with:

Spicy Peanut Sauce (page 256)
Creamy Caper Sauce (page 245)
Red Pepper Butter Sauce (page 247)
Mushroom Sherry Sauce (page 248)
Sauce Niçoise (page 246)
Brown Butter Sauce (page 249)
Classic Pesto (page 252)
Herbed Aioli (page 224)
Tartar Sauce (page 226)
Chipotle Mayonnaise (page 223)
Flavored Butter (page 236)

Cooking Methods

BAKING Baking can be done in a very hot oven (400° to 450°) for a short time, about 10 minutes per inch of thickness, or in a moderate oven (350° to 375°) for a longer time, but always preheat the oven, or the outside of the fish may be overdone before the inside is done. Bake the fish in an oiled pan, perfectly plain or brushed with butter or oil, drizzled with lemon juice, and seasoned.

BROILING & GRILLING Particularly good for fatty fish; lean fish should be basted with oil or butter. The goal in broiling and grilling is that the surfaces are nicely seared at the same time that the inside is cooked. The timing depends on how hot the broiler or grill is and how far the fish is from the heat. Do not broil cuts much thicker than an inch because the outside may become leathery before the inside is done.

PAN-FRYING & SAUTÉING Pan-fry fish in a skillet on medium-low heat, in a little butter or oil. Don't crowd the fish or use a lid because either will cause steam, which prevents browning and crisping. Pan-fry 1 inch-thick fish for about 4 minutes on each side.

Sauté fish in a skillet on medium-high heat in just enough oil to prevent sticking. Sautéing is very quick—the fish should be in and out of the pan in minutes.

For either method, fish should be dry when it goes into the pan. Dust the fish with a light coating of flour or cornmeal if you wish. When done, the skin will be crisp and the flesh moist and succulent. Season the fish after it's cooked.

POACHING Poach fish on the stovetop in enough water, broth, or wine and water to cover. Bring the liquid to a boil, add the fish, and reduce the heat to very gently simmer the fish for about 10 minutes per inch of thickness, until it loses its transparent look and flakes easily. Remove the fish with a slotted spoon.

To oven-poach, preheat the oven to 400°, place the fish in an oiled baking pan, add about a cup of liquid, and cover with foil. Cook until done, about 15 minutes for salmon fillets.

STEAMING Steaming liquid can be flavored with herbs, spices, and vegetables, or herbs and spices can be laid on top of and under the fish. Rub the fish with a light coating of oil and place it on a rack or heatproof plate inside a pot with a tight lid. Or you can steam the fish in a cheesecloth bag suspended in the steam like they do around the Chesapeake Bay. Steam fish for about 4 minutes per $1/2$ inch of thickness.

Choose the Freshest

With fish, freshness is all-important—more important, we think, than the kind or cut of the fish. Even when a recipe calls for a particular fish, we'll substitute whatever fish is freshest at the market that day, and it works out fine.

Your best bet for consistently good seafood is finding a market with knowledgeable and honest people behind the counter. Talk to them. Ask what they'll be taking home for dinner. They know the fish and know what's good. Sometimes the most reasonably priced fish is also the highest quality. (When a species is abundant, fishermen bring in their catches more often and the fish is shipped more quickly, making the price lower and the fish fresher when it gets to your market.) So when you shop for fish, instead of insisting on a particular kind, look for the best choice that day.

Trust your own judgment, too. Fresh fish has firm, elastic flesh and a clean, pleasant, deep-sea fragrance. Ask to smell the fish you're thinking about buying, and don't be shy about refusing it if the odor is disagreeable. Health regulations may forbid waving the fish itself under your nose, but you can get the same information by sniffing a tissue wiped across the fish.

Wild-Caught & Farm-Raised Issues

Choosing the best seafood while considering health and environmental issues can be daunting. Both farm-raised and wild-caught fish may contain contaminants, and some of the practices of both fish farming and wild harvesting have damaging environmental effects. Because of concerns about contamination, many fish farmers are looking for better methods, and some current practices, such as the establishment of mussel beds, are actually beneficial to the aquaculture. Ocean fishing practices change, too, often in an effort to protect depleted species. As for which fish to look for or to avoid, we can't make specific recommendations that we are sure will still be accurate at the time you read this, so our advice is that you keep abreast of the issues in your region so you can come to informed conclusions.

oven-roasted miso sesame salmon ∾

This salmon, quickly roasted, is moist and flavorful with its sweet-salty glaze of mirin and miso.

SERVES 4

TIME: 20 MINUTES

4 serving-sized pieces of salmon fillet (about 6 ounces each)
2 tablespoons light miso
1½ tablespoons mirin
1½ teaspoons brown sugar
2 tablespoons rice vinegar or cider vinegar
2 tablespoons toasted sesame seeds
chopped scallions

Preheat the oven to 450°. Rinse the salmon and place it skin-side down on an oiled baking sheet. With a sharp knife, make about 4 slashes across each fillet, taking care not to cut all the way through. In a small bowl, combine the miso, mirin, brown sugar, and vinegar.

Roast the salmon for 5 minutes. Remove it from the oven, spoon the miso-mirin glaze onto the fillets, and return it to the oven until the fish flakes easily with a fork but is still moist, 3 to 5 minutes, depending on the thickness of the fillets. Serve sprinkled with toasted sesame seeds and scallions.

INGREDIENT NOTE If you don't have mirin (page 290), increase the brown sugar to 1 tablespoon.

serving & menu ideas ∾

Serve on a bed of soba, rice, or wheat noodles or on rice (see page 176), with Pan-Asian Slaw (page 212) on the side. Leftovers are good flaked, in a vegetable sauté or on a salad.

seafood orzo ✎

Monkfish is perfect for this recipe because it doesn't fall apart. It has a wonderfully tender and succulent texture similar to lobster, but monkfish is less expensive. This dish is also good with other types of fish and other kinds of seafood, such as scallops, shrimp, or lobster.

SERVES 4

TIME: 35 MINUTES

1 28-ounce can of diced tomatoes
1 14-ounce can of clam broth
1 cup dry white wine
1 teaspoon salt
3 cups chopped onions
3 garlic cloves, pressed or minced
3 tablespoons olive oil
8 ounces orzo
$1/2$ pound monkfish
$1/2$ pound chopped clams or clam strips
3 tablespoons chopped fresh basil
$1/4$ teaspoon black pepper

In a covered saucepan, bring the tomatoes, clam broth, wine, and salt to a simmer.

Meanwhile, in a soup pot on medium heat, sauté the onions and garlic in the oil for 2 minutes. Add the orzo and cook, stirring constantly, until the orzo turns golden, about 3 minutes. Stir in the hot tomato mixture, cover, and cook on medium-low heat until the orzo is almost al dente, about 10 minutes.

Meanwhile, cut the monkfish into bite-sized chunks. When the orzo is barely al dente, add the monkfish, clams, basil, and pepper and cook until the fish is cooked all the way through, about 5 minutes.

serving & menu ideas ✎

Serve the rest of the bottle of wine with dinner. Add Caesar Salad without the Tofu Croutons (page 109) and Orange-Almond Polenta Cake (page 266) and you've got a dinner party!

moroccan spiced fish ↶

Any firm fish is fine for this intensely flavored and aromatic dish. If you use thick fillets, such as salmon or tuna, and you have the time, coat the fish with the spice mixture and then cover and refrigerate for an hour or two to marinate.

SERVES 4

HANDS-ON TIME:
15 MINUTES

BAKING TIME:
10 TO 15 MINUTES

3 tablespoons Moroccan Spice Mix (page 239)

2 garlic cloves, minced or pressed

2 tablespoons minced fresh cilantro

1 tablespoon olive oil

3 tablespoons lemon juice

1½ pounds fish fillets

Preheat the oven to 350°. In a bowl, stir together Moroccan Spice Mix and the garlic, cilantro, olive oil, and lemon juice. Rinse and pat dry the fish fillets, and cut them into chunks. Dredge the pieces of fish in the spice mixture and place them in an oiled baking dish. Spoon any spice mixture that's left over the top of the fish.

Bake uncovered for 10 to 15 minutes, until the fish is opaque and flaky but still moist.

serving & menu ideas ↶

This fish is absolutely delicious in a pita sandwich with shredded lettuce, chopped tomatoes, and lemony mayonnaise, Cilantro Yogurt Sauce (page 232), or plain yogurt. It also makes a great fish taco—wrap in tortillas with lettuce or finely sliced cabbage and tomatoes. Or serve it on rice or couscous with Roasted Sweet Potatoes (page 197) and a salad with Cilantro Lime Dressing (page 225). If you have leftovers, make a stew with onions, potatoes, peppers, zucchini, and tomatoes . . . and extra Moroccan Spice Mix.

flounder with herbed lemon butter ∾

*This is one of the fastest yet most delectable fish preparations.
Flounder is a delicate fish, so you need to use care (a wide
spatula helps) when turning it to cook on the second side.*

SERVES 2

TIME: 15 MINUTES

12 ounces flounder or sole fillets (4 fillets, each about 3 ounces)

¼ teaspoon salt

⅛ teaspoon black pepper

¼ cup unbleached white flour

1½ teaspoons olive oil

2 tablespoons butter

1 tablespoon lemon juice

1 tablespoon chopped fresh herbs, such as parsley, chives, dill,
  tarragon, or basil

lemon wedges

Rinse the fish and pat dry. Mix the salt and pepper with the flour in a shallow dish or a
large plate. Press the fish fillets into the flour to lightly coat. Shake off any excess flour.

On medium heat, warm a skillet large enough to hold all the fish. Add the olive oil and
1 tablespoon of the butter and swirl to coat the bottom. Add the fish and cook for 2 minutes for very thin fillets, 4 minutes for thicker ones. Turn the fillets and cook for a minute
or two on the second side. Turn off the heat and transfer the fish to a warm serving plate.

Add the remaining tablespoon of butter and the lemon juice and herbs to the skillet. The
pan should be hot enough to melt the butter, but if it isn't, return it to the heat for a
moment. Stir to incorporate the pan juices. Pour the herbed lemon butter over the fish
and serve at once with lemon wedges.

serving & menu ideas ∾

Serve with couscous or bulghur and Marmalade-Glazed Carrots (page 196). Another time,
serve with Yellow Rice (page 179) and Peas & Escarole (page 190) or Lemony Green
Beans (page 192). Or try with Potatoes with Lemon & Capers (page 195) and Broccoli
Slaw (page 208).

asian braised fish with greens ∿

This stovetop method of braising results in moist fish and a flavorful pan sauce to serve over noodles or rice.

SERVES 4

TIME: 30 MINUTES

1 pound soba or udon noodles or $1\frac{1}{2}$ cups jasmine, brown, or white rice

3 tablespoons soy sauce

3 tablespoons mirin or 2 tablespoons brown sugar

1 tablespoon rice vinegar

1 tablespoon grated peeled ginger root

3 garlic cloves, minced or pressed

6 scallions

1 head of bok choy (about $1\frac{1}{2}$ pounds)

$1\frac{1}{2}$ pounds firm fish fillets, at least $\frac{1}{2}$-inch thick

2 teaspoons vegetable oil

pinch of salt

sesame seeds (optional)

Cook the noodles or rice (see pages 16 and 176).

Meanwhile, in a bowl, combine the soy sauce, mirin, vinegar, ginger, garlic, and 3 tablespoons of water. Set aside. Cut the scallions on the diagonal into 1-inch pieces. Cut the bok choy on the diagonal into $\frac{1}{2}$-inch slices (about 8 cups). Cut the fish into serving-sized pieces or bite-sized chunks.

In a large skillet on high heat, stir-fry the scallions in the oil for a minute. Add the bok choy and salt. Stir constantly until the greens are just tender but still crisp, about 3 minutes. Transfer to a bowl and cover to keep warm.

Add the soy sauce mixture to the skillet and bring to a simmer. Add the fish fillets, cover, and simmer on low heat until cooked through: for fillets, about 6 minutes for each $\frac{1}{2}$ inch of thickness, and for chunks, about 4 minutes. Carefully turn over the fish about halfway through cooking. The fish is done when the flesh is opaque.

Serve the fish on a bed of the rice or noodles. Top with the bok choy, the pan sauce, and a sprinkling of sesame seeds.

pine nut-crusted fish ～

Breaded fish is one of our favorites. The richness of pine nuts nicely balances the lemon and herbs to make an irresistible dish. Use just about any fish: flounder, salmon, tilapia, perch, cod, snapper, catfish.

SERVES 4

TIME: 20 MINUTES

$\frac{1}{2}$ cup unseasoned bread crumbs

2 garlic cloves, minced or pressed

2 teaspoons dried oregano

1 tablespoon grated lemon peel

$\frac{1}{2}$ teaspoon salt

$\frac{1}{2}$ teaspoon black pepper

$\frac{1}{2}$ cup toasted pine nuts

1 egg

$1\frac{1}{2}$ pounds fish fillets

olive oil

In a blender or the bowl of a food processor, combine the bread crumbs, garlic, oregano, grated lemon peel, salt, and pepper, and process until well blended. Add the pine nuts and process until they are evenly chopped. Place the bread crumb mixture in a shallow bowl large enough to hold a single fish fillet. In another bowl, beat the egg.

Dip each fillet into the beaten egg and then coat each side with the bread crumb mixture. Place the breaded fillets on a piece of waxed paper or a plate.

Heat a large skillet and add about 2 tablespoons of olive oil. On medium heat, cook the fillets for about 4 minutes for every $\frac{1}{2}$ inch of thickness. Turn the fish and cook on the second side for an equal amount of time. If you need to cook the fish in batches, add more oil for each batch.

serving & menu ideas ～

Serve something fresh and colorful on the side: Tomatoes & Onions with Mint (page 205), Broccoli Tomato Salad (page 204), or Broccoli Slaw (page 208).

louisiana catfish with grits & greens ∾

For a simple supper, we can't imagine adding anything to this dish other than sliced tomatoes, zydeco music, and a little two-step.

SERVES 4

TIME: 35 MINUTES

GREENS

1 bunch collard greens or kale (about 1 pound)

2 garlic cloves, minced or pressed

1 teaspoon olive oil

$^1/_2$ teaspoon salt

1 teaspoon Tabasco or other hot pepper sauce, or more to taste

CHEESE GRITS

3 cups water

$^1/_2$ teaspoon salt

$^3/_4$ cup quick-cooking grits

$^1/_2$ cup grated Cheddar cheese

LOUISIANA CATFISH

4 catfish fillets (about 7 ounces each)

1 teaspoon paprika

$1^1/_2$ teaspoons dried oregano

1 teaspoon dried thyme

2 teaspoons brown sugar

$^1/_8$ teaspoon cayenne

1 teaspoon salt

1 teaspoon black pepper

2 tablespoons olive oil

To cook the greens: Rinse the greens. Remove and discard the large central stems. Coarsely chop the leaves to yield about 8 cups, lightly packed. In a pot large enough to hold the greens, cook the garlic in the oil for a minute and then add the salt, greens, and 2 tablespoons of water. Cover and cook on medium heat, stirring now and then, until the greens are tender, about 5 to 10 minutes. Add more water, if necessary, to prevent sticking. When the collards are tender, toss them with Tabasco. Cover and turn off the heat.

To make the grits: In a saucepan, bring the water and the salt to a boil. Add the grits in a slow, steady stream while stirring briskly. When the water returns to a boil, turn the heat down to very low, cover, and cook for about 10 minutes, stirring occasionally. When the grits are thickened and tender, stir in the cheese. Cover and turn off the heat.

To cook the catfish: Rinse and pat dry the fillets. Combine the paprika, oregano, thyme, brown sugar, cayenne, salt, and pepper on a plate. Press each fillet into the spice mixture to coat. In a skillet on medium to high heat, warm the oil and swirl to coat the bottom. Add the fish and cook for about 4 minutes for each ½ inch of thickness. Turn the fillets and cook the other side for about the same amount of time.

Serve the catfish hot from the pan with the collard greens and grits on the side.

INGREDIENT NOTES It's easy to strip fresh greens: Hold the base of a stem in one hand, grasp the bottom part of the leaf with your other hand, and pull the stem away from the leaf.

Quick-cooking grits are good, but instant grits should be shunned. Of course, old-fashioned longer-cooking grits are great if you have the time.

old bay roasted fish & vegetables ❧

Let your oven do the work on this juicy, piquant fish and the succulent red and orange roasted vegetables.

SERVES 4

TIME: 45 MINUTES

OLD BAY VEGETABLES

2 large sweet potatoes

1 large onion

1 large bell pepper, preferably red

3 tablespoons olive oil

1 teaspoon dried thyme

1 tablespoon Old Bay Seasoning

OLD BAY FISH

4 fish fillets (about 6 ounces each), such as tilapia, cod, or halibut

1 tablespoon olive oil

2 tablespoons lemon juice

2 garlic cloves, minced or pressed

1 tablespoon Old Bay Seasoning

Preheat the oven to 450°. Oil a baking sheet for the vegetables and a baking pan for the fish.

Peel the sweet potatoes and cut them in half lengthwise and then crosswise into slices about 1/3 inch thick. Peel the onion and cut it in half and then into 1/2-inch slices. Stem and seed the pepper and cut it into 1 1/2-inch chunks. In a mixing bowl, toss the vegetables with the oil and the thyme and Old Bay Seasoning. Spread on the baking sheet. Roast for 25 to 30 minutes, until the vegetables are tender and browned.

While the vegetables roast, place the fish fillets in a single layer in the baking pan. Whisk the oil with the lemon juice, garlic, and Old Bay Seasoning and drizzle over the fish.

When the vegetables have roasted for about 15 minutes, stir them with a spatula to prevent sticking. Put the pan of fish in the oven and bake until the fish flakes easily with a fork, about 10 minutes per inch of thickness.

shrimp curry with snow peas ∾

*Bright green snow peas and rosy shrimp in a creamy, golden
sauce—an elegant dish in only 20 minutes.
(See photo on page 150.)*

SERVES 4

TIME: 20 MINUTES

1 pound peeled and deveined large shrimp

1 large onion, thinly sliced (about 2 cups)

1 tablespoon vegetable oil

2 tablespoons Curry Powder (page 238)

5 ounces snow peas, cut in half on the diagonal (about 2 cups)

3 tomatoes, chopped (about 2 cups)

1 14-ounce can of coconut milk

½ teaspoon salt

2 tablespoons lemon or lime juice

¼ cup chopped fresh cilantro, basil, or Thai basil

If your shrimp is frozen, place it in cold water before you start. Because the shrimp cooks
in the coconut milk, it does not have to be completely defrosted.

In a saucepan on medium-high heat, sauté the onions in the oil for about 5 minutes, until
softened. Add the shrimp and Curry Powder and cook for a minute or two, stirring to prevent sticking. Add the snow peas and tomatoes and cook for a couple of minutes, and
turn the shrimp to cook on both sides. When the shrimp are mostly pink, pour in the
coconut milk, salt, and lemon or lime juice and bring to a simmer. Stir in the cilantro or
basil and add salt and pepper to taste. Serve hot.

variations ∾

Add a Keiffer lime leaf or two with the Curry Powder for a delicate yet distinctive flavor.

This generous sauce will hold more vegetables, so if you like, add baby corn, straw
mushrooms, chopped bell peppers, or fresh baby spinach.

serving & menu ideas ∾

Serve on plain rice, Lemongrass Rice (page 181), or Green Rice (page 180).

shrimp & avocado salad ∾

For a summer luncheon or a light supper, there's nothing better than this lovely salad dressed with lemon and tarragon.

SERVES 4

TIME: 20 MINUTES

1 pound peeled and deveined shrimp

2 tablespoons vegetable oil or olive oil

2 garlic cloves, minced or pressed

DRESSING

juice and zest of 1 lemon

1 tablespoon Dijon mustard

1 tablespoon chopped fresh tarragon

$1/2$ teaspoon salt

$1/4$ teaspoon black pepper

$1/2$ cup olive oil

2 avocados

2 tomatoes

6 cups baby greens or torn lettuce

If you're using frozen shrimp, begin to thaw it by placing it in cold water about 15 minutes before cooking.

Warm the oil in a skillet, add the garlic and shrimp, and sauté until the shrimp turn pink, 2 to 4 minutes. Set aside.

Whisk together the dressing ingredients. Toss the cooked shrimp with $1/4$ cup of the dressing. Peel and pit the avocados and cut into wedges. Cut the tomatoes into wedges. Arrange the shrimp, avocados, and tomatoes on the greens and drizzle on more of the dressing.

serving & menu ideas ∾

Pass extra dressing and bowls of olives, red onion slices, and cucumber slices at the table.

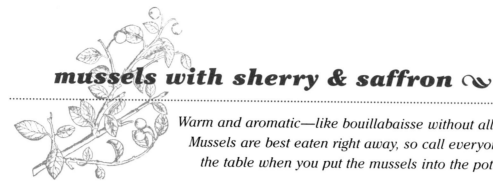

mussels with sherry & saffron ～

*Warm and aromatic—like bouillabaisse without all the fuss.
Mussels are best eaten right away, so call everyone to
the table when you put the mussels into the pot.*

SERVES 2 TO 4

TIME: 15 MINUTES

2 pounds cleaned and debearded fresh mussels

1 orange

1 tablespoon olive oil

3 garlic cloves, minced

$\frac{1}{2}$ cup sherry

pinch of saffron

$\frac{1}{2}$ teaspoon salt

sprinkling of black pepper

1 loaf of crusty French or Italian bread

In a colander, rinse the mussels with cold running water. Discard any mussels that are cracked or don't close when tapped. Grate the orange peel and juice the orange.

In a large pot with a lid, warm the olive oil on medium heat and cook the garlic for a minute. Add the sherry, $\frac{1}{2}$ cup of water, the orange zest and juice, saffron, salt, and pepper. Increase the heat, cover, and bring to a boil. Add the mussels, cover, and cook for 3 to 6 minutes, stirring once or twice, until the shells open. Discard any unopened mussels.

With a slotted spoon, place the mussels in soup bowls and then ladle the broth over. Serve with plenty of crusty bread to sop up the juices.

variations ～

Add chopped tomatoes and chopped parsley at the same time as the sherry.

After removing the mussels from the pot, stir $\frac{1}{2}$ cup of half-and-half or cream into the broth.

serving & menu ideas ～

Serve with a salad such as Baby Greens with Pecans & Pears (page 206).

seared scallops ∾

These sweet, delectable scallops are browned and caramelized on the outside, moist on the inside, and ready in an instant.

SERVES 4

TIME: 15 MINUTES

1 pound scallops
3 tablespoons olive oil
salt and pepper
lemon wedges

Rinse the scallops and pat dry with a paper towel. If they differ in size, cut the larger ones in half crosswise.

Heat the oil in a large skillet on high heat until the oil is very hot but not smoking. Add the scallops and stir gently to coat with oil. Sprinkle with salt and pepper. When the scallops have developed a brown crust, usually in 2 or 3 minutes, gently turn them over and cook until the other side is browned, 2 or 3 minutes. Transfer the scallops to a serving dish. Serve with lemon wedges.

INGREDIENT NOTE Ask for "dry" or untreated scallops, ones that have not been treated with STP solution (sodium tripolyphosphate), a preservative.

serving & menu ideas ∾

Serve on a bed of rice or baby spinach. These scallops are *really* good drizzled with Brown Butter Sauce (page 249). Try them with Brilliant Yellow Noodles (page 185) and Wilted Spinach Salad with Pecans & Asiago (page 215) for a vibrant supper.

crisp pan-fried scallops ∾

These scallops are pan-fried, but the effect is very similar to deep-fried. Panko crumbs or flakes are Japanese-style bread crumbs. They're coarser and more irregularly shaped than regular bread crumbs, and although they look fresh, they're dry. When used for frying, they absorb less oil and make a lighter, crunchier, more tender and delicate coating that stays crisp longer than ordinary coatings.

SERVES 4

TIME: 15 MINUTES

1 pound scallops
1 egg
2 tablespoons milk
$\frac{1}{2}$ teaspoon salt
$\frac{1}{8}$ teaspoon black pepper
$1\frac{1}{2}$ cups panko
$\frac{1}{4}$ cup vegetable oil
lemon wedges

Rinse the scallops and pat dry. If they differ in size, cut the larger ones in half crosswise. In a bowl, whisk the egg with the milk, salt, and pepper. Add the scallops and toss gently to coat. Spread the panko on a flat plate and generously coat each scallop.

Heat the oil in a large skillet on medium-high heat until the oil is hot but not smoking. Carefully add about half of the scallops, one at a time. Cook on the first side for 3 or 4 minutes, until golden brown. (If the panko is browning too quickly, reduce the heat.) Turn over the scallops with tongs and cook on the other side until golden brown, about 3 minutes. Place the cooked scallops on paper towels to soak up extra oil. Fry the rest of the scallops. Serve with lemon wedges.

INGREDIENT NOTES Look for panko in bags or boxes in Asian markets or supermarkets. We often use Sun Luck brand, but any brand with good ingredients is fine.

Ask for "dry" or untreated scallops, ones that have not been treated with STP solution (sodium tripolyphosphate), a preservative.

serving & menu ideas ∾

Serve on a bed of rice with a steamed green vegetable, Peas & Escarole (page 190), or refreshing Carrot Salad with Raspberry Vinaigrette (page 217).

po' boy sandwich ∾

*We've come to love Old Bay seasoning for its aromatic flavor.
(See photo on page 227.)*

SERVES 4

TIME: 30 MINUTES

FISH FILLETS

¼ cup cornmeal

3 tablespoons Old Bay Seasoning or other seafood seasoning

4 boneless firm fish fillets (about 6 ounces each)

¼ cup vegetable oil

TOPPING

½ cup Tartar Sauce (page 226)

1 tablespoon minced red onions

3 romaine lettuce leaves, cut into a rough shred

4 kaiser or sub rolls

1 tomato

Place the cornmeal and Old Bay seasoning in a bag and shake to mix well. Add the fish fillets, close the bag, and shake to coat. (Or mix the cornmeal and seasoning on a plate and press the fish into it to coat.) Heat the oil in a skillet on medium-high heat, until hot but not smoking. Add the fish and cook for 3 to 4 minutes on each side or until the fish flakes easily when tested with a fork. Place the cooked fish on paper towels to soak up excess oil.

While the fish is frying, in a bowl, stir together the Tartar Sauce and onions, add the lettuce, and toss until evenly coated. Toast the rolls and slice the tomato.

To make the sandwiches, place a fish fillet on the bottom half of each roll. Spoon on some topping, add tomato slices, and cap with the top half of the roll.

serving & menu ideas ∾

Serve with plenty of napkins and a cold drink—and then Peach Brown Betty (page 268) or Banana Cupcakes (page 274).

newport sardine sandwich ∾

An open-faced sandwich that cries out for a glass of cold lemonade or beer.

SERVES 2

TIME: 15 MINUTES

3 slices of whole wheat or rye bread
1 tablespoon mayonnaise
1 tablespoon mustard
1 small mild onion, such as Bermuda or Vidalia, thinly sliced
1 3.75-ounce can of sardines packed in oil
2 small tomatoes, sliced

Toast the bread until quite crisp. Mix the mayonnaise and mustard and spread on the toast. Top with onion slices. With a fork, lift sardines from the can and put them on the onions. Then use the fork to lightly mash the sardines to cover the onions.

With a sharp knife, cut each sandwich on the diagonal into fourths. Top each piece with a tomato slice.

variations ∾

Try topping the sandwiches with sliced or grated Swiss, Monterey Jack, or Cheddar cheese and pop them under the broiler to melt the cheese.

serving & menu ideas ∾

A bowl of Tomato Tortilla Soup (page 117) would be perfect with this sandwich.

*From top: Yellow Rice (page 179), Green Rice (page 180),
Lemongrass Rice (page 181), Coconut Rice (page 182)*

side grains

cooking plain grains

We love the variety of grains available to us—rice of all kinds, quinoa, bulghur, couscous, grits, kasha, and polenta. Grains are nutritious and filling and make wonderful beds for stews, curries, and bean, tofu, fish, and vegetable dishes. We suggest that you cook extra; leftover grains are invaluable on busy weekday nights. Top a green salad with them to make it more substantial. Add vegetables and/or dried fruit and nuts for a pilaf. Mix with herbs and cheese to stuff peppers or tomatoes. Add an egg and chopped vegetables and sprinkle with soy sauce for fried rice. Stir into a brothy soup. The possibilities go on and on—leftovers rarely languish in the refrigerator. Here are directions for cooking some of our favorite grains for simple suppers:

BULGHUR is made from wheat berries that have been steamed or parboiled, dried, and cracked. It is a quick-cooking, nutty-flavored grain. Medium and light bulghurs cook faster than coarser varieties. See Saucy Hungarian Eggplant (page 40) for cooking directions.

COUSCOUS is precooked semolina milled from durum wheat. It looks like tiny yellow irregularly shaped pearls. Whole wheat couscous is the same size and shape but with a light brown color and nuttier flavor. Couscous cooks quickly; put equal amounts of couscous and boiling water in a bowl with a little salt and olive oil, cover, and let sit until tender, about 5 minutes. Stir to fluff the grains.

GRITS are made from dried corn with the germ removed. Yellow and white grits have similar sweetness, flavor, and nutritional value. We recommend quick-cooking or regular grits but *not* instant grits, which contain additives and have an insipid flavor. Stone-ground grits are dried whole kernels of white or yellow corn crushed between millstones; they're delicious but take longer to cook than regular or quick-cooking. See Louisiana Catfish with Grits & Greens (page 162) for cooking directions.

KASHA is the common name for roasted buckwheat groats. It has a distinct earthy flavor and texture and looks like dark brown seeds. Kasha pairs well with mushrooms, onions, and root vegetables. See Kasha & Orzo with Portabellas (page 100) for a delectable example of how to enjoy kasha.

POLENTA is the Italian word for corn. Polenta can be made with any grind of cornmeal; the amount of water needed, the cooking time, and the texture of the finished polenta varies. Fast-cooking polenta cornmeal is finely ground, often cooks in just 5 minutes, generally does well with a 4:1 water to cornmeal ratio, and is smooth and creamy. Regular cornmeal does better with a 3:1 water to cornmeal ratio and needs to simmer for about 15 minutes. See page 184 for cooking and serving suggestions.

QUINOA *(KEEN-wah)* is an easily digested grain, first cultivated by the Incas and now widely available in this country. It has a mild, nutty flavor. Before cooking, thoroughly rinse it to remove the slightly bitter coating on the grains. It expands four to five times when cooked, so a little goes a long way. See Quinoa & Vegetable Pilaf (page 98) for a delicious recipe that uses this ancient grain.

Rice

ARBORIO RICE is an Italian short-grain, highly absorbent, starchy white rice used in risottos. Look for arborio rice, often called *riso* or risotto rice, in the ethnic section of the supermarket or in Italian specialty shops. We like brands imported from Italy and Rice Select brand Risotto: Italian-style Rice, which is grown in the United States. See pages 89–92 for some great risotto recipes.

BASMATI RICE is a fragrant rice, originally grown in the foothills of the Himalayas and now grown in the United States as well (domestic basmati is sometimes called Texmati or Calmati). Cook brown basmati like brown rice but with a little more water. To cook white basmati, rinse the rice and drain. Bring water (1¾ cups water to 1 cup rice) to a boil. Add salt and a little oil or butter, stir in the rice, lower the heat, cover, and simmer until the water is absorbed, about 15 minutes. Or, follow the instructions for white rice.

BROWN RICE has a chewy texture and excellent flavor. Only the hull is removed; the bran and germ are retained. It is available in long-, medium-, and short-grain varieties—the shorter the grain, the more plump and moist the cooked kernels are. Use long-grain when a fluffy rice is preferred. To cook brown rice, rinse and drain the rice, put it in a pot, stir it with a little oil and salt, add cool water (2 cups water to 1 cup rice, but less water for larger amounts: 4½ cups water to 3 cups rice), cover, and bring to a boil. As soon as the water boils, lower the heat and simmer until the water is absorbed, about 40 minutes.

JASMINE RICE is a fragrant, creamy, long-grain Thai rice. See the cooking directions for white rice.

WHITE RICE is also known as polished rice because it is processed to remove both its hull and bran. Enriched white rice has thiamine, niacin, and iron added. It comes in long-grain, medium-grain, and short-grain varieties. Cook white rice like brown rice but with less water (1¾ cups water to 1 cup rice) and significantly less simmering time (12 to 15 minutes).

yellow rice ❧

SERVES 4

TIME: 25 MINUTES

SIMMERING TIME:
15 MINUTES

1½ cups white rice

1 teaspoon vegetable oil

1 teaspoon turmeric or a generous pinch of saffron

2¼ cups water

½ teaspoon salt

Rinse and drain the rice. Heat the oil in a saucepan with a tight-fitting lid. Add the rice and turmeric or saffron and stir on high heat for a minute or two. Add the water and salt, cover, and bring to a boil on high heat. Lower the heat to a gentle simmer and cook covered for 12 to 15 minutes, or until all of the water is absorbed. Fluff the rice with a fork, cover, and let sit until ready to serve.

INGREDIENT NOTE Brown rice is fine in this recipe; it just takes longer to cook, about 40 minutes of simmering.

serving & menu ideas ❧

Yellow Rice is the perfect bed for Black Beans with Pickled Red Onions (page 58), West Indian Red Beans (page 69), Shrimp Curry with Snow Peas (page 165), Roasted Vegetable Curry (page 53), and Flounder with Herbed Lemon Butter (page 159).

green rice ॐ

SERVES 4

TIME: 25 MINUTES

SIMMERING TIME:
15 MINUTES

1½ cups white rice

1 tablespoon vegetable oil or olive oil

2¼ cups water

½ teaspoon salt

3 scallions

4 cups loosely packed spinach (about 3 ounces)

pinch of black pepper

Rinse and drain the rice. In a saucepan with a tight-fitting lid, on high heat briefly sauté the rice in 1 teaspoon of the oil, stirring to coat each grain. Add the water and salt, bring to a boil, cover, and reduce the heat to very low. Cook until the water is absorbed, about 12 to 15 minutes.

While the rice cooks, coarsely chop the scallions and rinse the spinach. In a large skillet, sauté the scallions in 2 teaspoons of the oil for a minute or two. Add the spinach and pepper, cover, and cook until just wilted and still bright green, about 2 minutes. In a blender, purée the spinach and scallions until smooth, adding a little water, if necessary.

When the rice is done, fluff it with a fork, stir in the spinach purée, and serve.

INGREDIENT NOTES This recipe is just fine with brown rice (see page 178), but it will take a bit longer to cook and the green color will be muted.

Add fresh herbs to the blender: about 2 tablespoons of dill, basil, or tarragon.

serving & menu ideas ॐ

Green Rice is pretty served under Scrambled Tofu with Greens & Raspberry Chipotle Sauce (page 67), Baked Stuffed Tomatoes (page 49), or Shrimp Curry with Snow Peas (page 165). Or top it with Easy Baked Tofu (page 64) or sautéed shrimp. Leftovers can become tomorrow's Green Fried Rice (page 96).

lemongrass rice ∾

SERVES 4

TIME: 30 MINUTES

SIMMERING TIME:
15 MINUTES

1 stalk fresh lemongrass

1½ cups jasmine or white basmati rice

1 teaspoon vegetable oil

2½ cups water

1 Keiffer lime leaf (optional)

½ teaspoon salt

Remove any dried outer leaves from the lemongrass stalk, cut it in half lengthwise, and mash the halves a bit with a mallet or the flat side of a large knife blade cut into lengths that fit in your pan and set aside.

Rinse and drain the rice. In a heavy saucepan with a tight-fitting lid, sauté the rice in the oil for a minute, stirring to coat the grains. Add the water, lime leaf, mashed lemongrass, and salt and bring to a boil on high heat. Reduce the heat to very low, cover, and simmer until the water is absorbed, 12 to 15 minutes. Remove and discard the lemongrass and lime leaf. Fluff the rice with a fork.

serving & menu ideas ∾

Great with curries, sautés, and fish or tofu dishes, or as the base for fried rice. Serve this fragrant rice under Curried Tofu with Tomatoes (page 44), or Roasted Sweet Potatoes (page 197) and Easy Baked Tofu (page 64). Turn leftovers into Pineapple Fried Rice with Tofu (page 88).

coconut rice

SERVES 4 TO 6

TIME: 25 MINUTES

SIMMERING TIME:
15 TO 20 MINUTES

$1\frac{1}{2}$ cups white rice

$\frac{1}{2}$ teaspoon turmeric

$\frac{1}{2}$ teaspoon salt

1 teaspoon vegetable oil

$1\frac{1}{2}$ cups water

$\frac{3}{4}$ cup coconut milk

Rinse and drain the rice. In a saucepan on medium-high heat, sauté the rice, turmeric, and salt in the oil for a minute or two, stirring constantly. Add the water and coconut milk, bring to a boil, cover, and reduce the heat to low. Simmer until the rice is tender and the liquid absorbed, 15 to 20 minutes.

serving & menu ideas ∾

This sweet rice perfectly complements West Indian Red Beans (page 69), Sesame Tofu with Spinach (page 56), or Spicy Potatoes & Spinach (page 45) with Cranberry Chutney (page 231) on the side.

Cranberry Bulghur Pilaf (opposite)

cranberry bulghur pilaf ∿

SERVES 4 TO 6

TIME: 30 MINUTES

2 tablespoons olive oil

1½ cups chopped onions

3 garlic cloves, pressed or minced

dash of salt

1 orange

½ teaspoon crumbled dried rosemary (1½ teaspoons
   chopped fresh)

1½ cups medium to light bulghur

1½ cups water or vegetable broth (see page 295)

½ cup dried cranberries (or currants or raisins)

1 tablespoon soy sauce

1 tablespoon lemon juice

⅔ cup chopped toasted pecans, walnuts, or almonds (optional)

In a saucepan on medium heat, warm the oil, add the onions and garlic, sprinkle with salt, and cook until softened, about 10 minutes. While the onions cook, grate the orange peel and juice the orange.

Add the rosemary, orange zest, and bulghur to the onions and cook for a minute, stirring. Add the orange juice, water or vegetable broth, and dried cranberries, cover, and cook on low heat until all the liquid is absorbed, about 10 minutes. If the bulghur is still crunchy, add ¼ cup of hot water and cook for a few minutes longer. Remove from the heat. Stir in the soy sauce and lemon juice. Add nuts if you like, and more soy sauce and/or lemon juice to taste.

INGREDIENT NOTE If you don't have a fresh orange, you could use ½ cup of prepared orange juice.

serving & menu ideas ∿

Serve with Easy Baked Tofu (page 64) or Seared Scallops (page 169).

polenta ∾

*Polenta can be made with any grind of cornmeal. We call for
polenta cornmeal because it makes a particularly smooth
and creamy polenta that also cooks quickly.*

SERVES 4 TO 6

TIME: 10 MINUTES

4 cups water

1 teaspoon salt

1 cup polenta cornmeal

1 or 2 tablespoons olive oil or butter

Bring the water and salt to a rapid boil in a heavy-bottomed pot. Slowly pour in the corn-meal, whisking constantly to prevent lumps. Lower the heat and simmer, stirring often, until the polenta thickens and tastes done, about 5 minutes. Whisk in the oil or butter.

variations ∾

The mild corn flavor of polenta makes it a good vehicle for other flavors. Add any of these to the boiling water: 4 or 5 chopped sun-dried tomatoes, a teaspoon of ground fennel seeds or dried thyme or rosemary, ¼ teaspoon of red pepper flakes, 2 teaspoons of ground cumin, or a tablespoon of chopped garlic. At the end, whisk in grated cheese and/or chopped fresh herbs.

POLENTA CUTLETS Polenta thickens as it cools, making it great for baked breaded "cutlets" that are crisp on the outside and creamy on the inside, good topped with tomato sauce. To make cutlets, pour hot polenta into an oiled baking dish to a depth of about an inch. Refrigerate until cold. Cut into squares, rectangles, or triangles. Dip each piece into beaten eggs, milk, or water and then coat with plain or seasoned fine bread crumbs. Bake at 400° for 10 or 15 minutes on each side.

serving & menu ideas ∾

Polenta is perfect for many dishes—chunky stews, beans, sautéed greens, and roasted vegetables. We like it with White Bean & Mushroom Ragout (page 73), Roasted Ratatouille (page 50), Mushroom Sherry Sauce (page 248), and Simple Tomato Sauce (page 251).

brilliant yellow noodles ᔑ

Always a kid-friendly choice.

SERVES 4

TIME: 15 TO
25 MINUTES

3 quarts water

1½ teaspoons turmeric

1 teaspoon salt

12 ounces pasta, any shape

Bring the water to a boil. Stir in the turmeric and salt and then add the pasta. Cook until the pasta is al dente, stirring occasionally. Drain and serve.

INGREDIENT NOTE For this recipe, we've used Italian pasta, spelt pasta, rice noodles, and egg noodles.

serving & menu ideas ᔑ

These bright yellow noodles are fun simply topped with your favorite pasta sauce or vegetable sauté. Use leftovers in a pasta salad. Serve under Tofu & Mushrooms Marsala (page 70), Spring Vegetable Sauté (page 38), or instead of bulghur with Saucy Hungarian Eggplant (page 40).

Peppercorn Citrus Marinated Feta (page 201)

side dishes

corn on the cob ∾

Nothing beats fresh corn on the cob at the height of summer. When local corn is harvested, we want to eat it almost every day—seizing the moment, celebrating the season, getting it while we can. Flavorful toppings can keep this seasonal treat interesting. And when fresh corn on the cob is out of season, any of the toppings are good stirred into heated and drained frozen or canned corn kernels.

Cooking Corn on the Cob

BOILING In a large pot of boiling water, cook very tender young ears of shucked corn just until hot, a minute or less, and more mature ears no more than 3 to 5 minutes.

STEAMING Remove the coarse outer husks, leaving the silk and more tender inner husks in place. (The husks help steam the kernels.) In a steamer on the stovetop, place the ears uncrowded in a single layer or standing upright. Depending on the size of the steamer and how closely the corn is packed, steam for 5 to 10 minutes, until the corn is hot and tender. In a microwave oven, you can steam one or two ears of corn at a time. Cook unshucked ears at the highest setting for about 2 minutes per ear. After steaming, most of the silk will come off when you peel back the husks.

GRILLING Choose large ears of corn with plump kernels. Grill right on the rack about 4 inches above glowing coals. Turn several times during cooking. Grill bare ears for 3 to 5 minutes and unshucked ears for 8 to 10 minutes.

Corn on the Cob Toppings

Boil, steam, or grill the corn and then slather on a topping:

FLAVORED BUTTER (page 236)

CHIPOTLE MAYONNAISE (page 223)

RED PEPPER BUTTER SAUCE (page 247)

TEX-MEX STYLE

Spread mayonnaise on the hot corn and then dribble on (or drench with) Tabasco or other hot pepper sauce, and lime juice and sprinkle with grated Parmesan cheese.

CHESAPEAKE BAY STYLE

Stir Old Bay Seasoning and lemon juice into melted butter or oil.

SPICY TOPPINGS

∽ Stir lime or lemon juice and a pinch of cayenne into melted butter or olive oil.

∽ Use your favorite barbecue sauce straight from the bottle.

∽ Try equal parts maple syrup and melted butter, with minced canned chipotles in adobo sauce (see page 286) stirred in.

∽ Stir freshly grated orange zest and chili powder or Tabasco or other hot pepper sauce into melted butter.

serving & menu ideas ∽

Of course, corn on the cob is always the star of the backyard summer supper. Next time, make the usual picnic dishes, but with a twist: Chipotle Potato Salad (page 216) and Pan-Asian Slaw (page 212) and one of the corn on the cob toppings new to you. Corn on the cob is also great in unexpected combinations: Follow Indonesian Sweet Potato & Cabbage Soup (page 122) with a big platter of corn on the cob with lime.

peas & escarole ∽

This quick side dish is so green and fresh-tasting that it seems the essence of spring, although with a package of frozen green peas, you can make it any time of year. Peas and escarole enhance each other wonderfully because of their contrasting tastes and textures.

SERVES 4 TO 6

TIME: 10 MINUTES

1 10-ounce package of frozen petite sweet peas (2 cups)
1 8-ounce head of escarole
1 tablespoon olive oil or butter
generous pinches of salt, black pepper, and sugar

Defrost the peas by placing them in a colander and running hot tap water over them for a minute. Thoroughly rinse the escarole and cut it into fine shreds (about 4 cups).

In a skillet on medium heat, sauté the escarole in the oil or butter for a minute or two, until bright green and wilted. Add the peas, salt, pepper, and sugar and cook, stirring constantly, just until the peas are hot, a minute or two.

serving & menu ideas ∽

So green and sweet, this is the perfect side dish for Flounder with Herbed Lemon Butter (page 159). Or serve it with Yellow Rice (page 179) and Lemon Herb Tofu (page 68). It's a delicious simple meal spooned on Polenta (page 184) or tossed with a chunky pasta and sprinkled with grated Parmesan.

apples two ways ∿

Sautéed on the stovetop or baked in the oven, these cinnamony apples add a sweet note to any meal. If you're already baking something for dinner, pop some apples into the oven too, and if the oven temperature is hotter or cooler, don't worry—just adjust the baking time.

sautéed apples

SERVES 2 TO 4

TIME: 15 TO 20 MINUTES

2 firm tart apples
1 tablespoon butter
2 tablespoons sugar
1 teaspoon cinnamon

Peel, core, and slice or dice the apples.

Melt the butter in a skillet on medium-high heat, add the apples, and sauté for 5 minutes, stirring often. Add the cinnamon and sugar and cook, stirring occasionally, until the apples are tender. Add a splash of water or juice while the apples are cooking if they stick to the skillet.

baked apples

SERVES 2 TO 4

HANDS-ON TIME: 5 MINUTES

BAKING TIME: 15 TO 20 MINUTES

2 firm tart apples
2 tablespoons sugar
1 teaspoon cinnamon

Preheat the oven to 400°. Cut the apples in half and core them. Place the halves cut-side down in an oiled baking dish. Bake until tender, 15 to 20 minutes.

While the apples bake, mix together the sugar and cinnamon. When the apples are done, turn them over and sprinkle with the sugar mixture.

serving & menu ideas ∿

Put some apples in the oven to bake with Roasted Vegetable Curry (page 53), Two Potato Gratin (page 48), or Green & White Bean Gratin (page 57). Or top vanilla ice cream with these apples while they are still hot. Serve leftover apples for breakfast on oatmeal or yogurt.

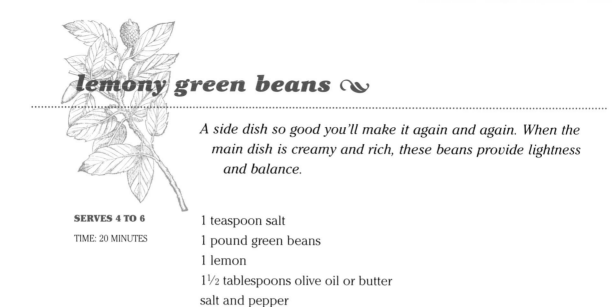

lemony green beans ∾

A side dish so good you'll make it again and again. When the main dish is creamy and rich, these beans provide lightness and balance.

SERVES 4 TO 6

TIME: 20 MINUTES

1 teaspoon salt
1 pound green beans
1 lemon
1½ tablespoons olive oil or butter
salt and pepper

In a covered saucepan, bring 3 or 4 inches of water and the salt to a boil. Rinse the green beans and trim the stem ends. When the water boils, add the green beans and cook until tender, 5 to 7 minutes.

While the beans are cooking, grate the lemon peel (see page 290) and juice the lemon and set aside. (You'll need 1½ tablespoons of lemon juice and about 1½ teaspoons of lemon zest.)

When the beans are tender, drain them and return them to the pan. Add the olive oil or butter and the lemon juice and toss to coat. Add salt and pepper to taste. Serve sprinkled with the lemon zest.

serving & menu ideas ∾

In late August or early September, when the local farmers' market reaches its peak, we like to make a vegetables-only meal: Lemony Green Beans, Potatoes with Lemon & Capers (page 195), Broccoli Tomato Salad (page 204), and Baked Acorn Squash Crescents (page 198).

sesame broccoli ∽

A light vinegar and dark sesame oil dressing brightens the flavor of broccoli. The sesame dressing is also delicious on other vegetables, such as bok choy, green beans, carrots, and asparagus.

SERVES 4

TIME: 15 MINUTES

1 teaspoon vinegar
2 teaspoons dark sesame oil
¼ teaspoon red pepper flakes (optional)
¼ teaspoon salt
1 bunch broccoli (about 1 pound)

In a small bowl, whisk together the vinegar, sesame oil, red pepper flakes, and salt. Cut the broccoli head into florets. Peel the large stems and cut them crosswise into ¼-inch slices. Steam or boil until crisp-tender. Toss the warm broccoli with the dressing. Serve warm or at room temperature.

INGREDIENT NOTE Use rice vinegar, white vinegar, or cider vinegar.

serving & menu ideas ∽

Sesame Broccoli is just right with Pineapple Fried Rice with Tofu (page 88), Crisp Pan-Fried Scallops (page 170), or noodles dressed with Spicy Peanut Sauce (page 256).

potatoes with lemon & capers ∾

After you taste these perfectly seasoned potatoes, you'll never go back to butter-drenched ones.

SERVES 4

TIME: 20 MINUTES

4 or 5 potatoes (about 1¾ pound)
1 lemon
1 tablespoon drained capers, more to taste
2 tablespoons olive oil
salt and pepper to taste

Bring 2 quarts of salted water to a boil. While the water heats, peel or scrub the potatoes and cut them into 1-inch cubes (about 4 cups). Add the potatoes to the water, return to a boil, and cook until a knife easily pierces but doesn't crumble a potato cube, about 5 minutes.

While the potatoes cook, grate the peel of the lemon (see page 290) into a large bowl, taking care to grate just the yellow part and not the white pith, which is bitter. Squeeze the lemon and add 2 tablespoons of the juice to the bowl. Add the capers, chopped if you wish.

Drain the cooked potatoes, add them to the bowl, drizzle on the oil, and toss. Add salt and pepper to taste.

serving & menu ideas ∾

Make extra so you'll have leftovers: a divine side dish the first day, and later a truly delectable potato salad, chilled, with mayonnaise stirred in. Serve on the side of Greek Frittata (page 78), Veggie Western Omelet (page 76), Flounder with Herbed Lemon Butter (page 159), or any dish that *needs* some potatoes.

marmalade-glazed carrots ∾

Made ahead and warmed up just before serving, these glazed carrots retain their color and flavor beautifully. A splash of lemon juice cuts the sweetness just a bit.

SERVES 4

TIME: 15 TO 20 MINUTES

3 cups peeled and cut carrots ($\frac{1}{2}$-inch slices)
1 tablespoon vegetable oil or butter
$\frac{3}{4}$ teaspoon salt
$\frac{1}{4}$ cup water
$\frac{1}{4}$ cup orange marmalade
lemon wedges

In a large skillet on medium-high heat, cook the carrots in the oil for about 2 minutes, stirring occasionally. Add the salt and water and continue to cook for 3 or 4 minutes, until the carrots are crisp-tender. Add the orange marmalade and stir until the carrots are well coated and glistening. Serve with lemon wedges.

serving & menu ideas ∾

These carrots are a sweet and colorful side next to Lemony Couscous with Chickpeas (page 97), Flounder with Herbed Lemon Butter (page 159), Warm French Lentil Salad (page 112) . . . and almost everything else!

roasted sweet potatoes ~

Roasting intensifies the natural sugars in sweet potatoes. These sweeter sweet potatoes come out of the oven soft in the center and crisp around the edges.

SERVES 4

HANDS-ON TIME:
10 MINUTES

BAKING TIME:
15 MINUTES

2½ pounds sweet potatoes

2 tablespoons olive oil

1 teaspoon salt

black pepper

Preheat the oven to 450°. Lightly oil a baking sheet.

Peel the sweet potatoes and slice them into rounds about ½ inch thick. If the potatoes are large, cut them in half lengthwise and then into half-rounds. (You should have 7 or 8 cups.) In a bowl, toss the sweet potatoes with the oil, salt, and a dash of pepper.

Spread the sweet potatoes on the prepared baking sheet in a single layer and roast for 10 minutes. Stir, and return to the oven until they are tender and beginning to brown, about 5 minutes.

serving & menu ideas ~

Delicious with Chipotle Scrambled Eggs (page 84) or Pine Nut–Crusted Fish (page 161). For a colorful meal with interesting contrasts, serve alongside Chipotle Tofu (page 65) and Corn & Pepper Salad (page 207).

baked acorn squash crescents ∾

These crescents are perfect simple supper fare; there's hardly any prep time involved, and while they bake, you can make the rest of the meal.

SERVES 2 TO 4

TIME: 30 MINUTES

1 acorn squash
2 tablespoons melted butter
2 tablespoons brown sugar
sprinkling of nutmeg or cinnamon (optional)

Preheat the oven to 400°. Lightly butter a 9 x 13-inch baking pan. Using a long sharp knife, cut the squash in half lengthwise. Remove the seeds and cut each half crosswise into ½-inch slices. Arrange the squash slices in a single layer in the prepared baking pan.

Bake for 15 minutes, until softened. With a spatula, turn over the squash slices and brush on the melted butter. Sprinkle with brown sugar and with nutmeg or cinnamon if you wish. Return to the oven for 5 minutes.

INGREDIENT NOTES In place of brown sugar, you can use maple syrup. Add it to the melted butter.

To safely cut a whole acorn squash in half, place it on a cutting board, finding the best position to avoid rolling. Use a long sharp knife. With both hands on the knife, one grasping the handle and the other flat (fingers straight) on the tip end cushioned with a pot holder or towel, place the center of the blade lengthwise along the middle of the squash. Lean onto the knife, using your body weight for leverage, and cut through the squash, making sure all of your fingers stay above the blade.

serving & menu ideas ∾

Try next to Cranberry Bulghur Pilaf (page 183), Sesame Tofu with Spinach (page 56), or Moroccan Spiced Fish (page 157), to name just a few good pairings.

miso-glazed eggplant ∾

This way of cooking eggplant makes the flesh soft and creamy.
The miso glaze sweetens it with a Japanese flair.

SERVES 6

TIME: 40 MINUTES

MARINADE

2 tablespoons sherry

1 tablespoon soy sauce

1 tablespoon peanut oil or vegetable oil

3 small thin eggplants, 5 or 6 inches long (about 1¼ pounds)

GLAZE

1 tablespoon sugar

1 tablespoon rice vinegar or cider vinegar

¼ cup light miso

1 tablespoon sesame seeds, whole or ground

Preheat the oven to 400°. Whisk together the marinade ingredients.

Cut the eggplants in half lengthwise, leaving the stems on. Using a sharp paring knife, score the flesh of each half in a crosshatch pattern, taking care not to puncture the skin. Place cut-side up on an oiled baking pan. Drizzle marinade over the eggplant halves. Cover with foil and bake until tender to the touch, 15 to 20 minutes.

Meanwhile, to prepare the glaze, stir the sugar and vinegar into the miso.

When the eggplant halves are tender, remove them from the oven, spread generously with the glaze, and sprinkle on the sesame seeds. Return them to the oven and bake, uncovered, for about 5 minutes more. Serve hot, warm, or at room temperature.

serving & menu ideas ∾

Serve Miso-Glazed Eggplant on rice or noodles with Easy Baked Tofu (page 64) and a spinach salad. For a snack, scoop out the soft interior with a spoon and serve with crackers. To make a meal of it, add Mushroom Miso Soup (page 128).

peppercorn citrus marinated feta ∾

Sour citrus and spicy peppercorns are perfect foils for salty feta.
(See photo on page 186.)

SERVES 6

TIME: 10 MINUTES

1 8-ounce block of feta cheese

16 black peppercorns

1 lemon

2 tablespoons olive oil (extra-virgin is nice)

Slice the block of feta into ¼-inch slabs and then into wide strips. Place on a plate or in a shallow serving bowl.

Crush the peppercorns. Place them on a cutting board and press down hard on them with a flat-bottomed pan (a pie plate works well), rocking the pan back and forth. You can use a peppermill or already cracked black pepper, but the freshly crushed peppercorns are really nice. Lightly grate the lemon peel (see page 290) and then juice the lemon.

To make the marinade, mix 2 teaspoons of the zest and 2 teaspoons of the juice with the olive oil and the crushed peppercorns. Drizzle the marinade over the feta and toss gently. You can eat the feta right away, but it's even better when marinated at room temperature for 30 minutes or more.

serving & menu ideas ∾

To tide you over until supper is ready, serve marinated feta with crackers, wedges of toasted pita or bread, and fresh fruit. Marinated feta is a good topping for Pasta with Olives Piquant (page 19) or fish with Sauce Niçoise (page 246). Make a Mediterranean-style summer meal of marinated feta and Sicilian Chickpea Spread (page 254) with crusty bread and olives and tomato and cucumber slices. And, of course, it's delicious on tossed green salads, too.

Carrot Salad with Raspberry Vinaigrette (page 217)

side salads

broccoli tomato salad ∾

*This vitamin-rich salad pairs well with an unfussy egg dish,
seafood, or cheesy pasta. It can be a very simple salad, or
dress it up with extras and make it into a meal on its own.*

SERVES 4 TO 6

TIME: 15 MINUTES

12 ounces broccoli crowns

2 tomatoes

⅓ cup olive oil (extra-virgin is nice)

2 tablespoons balsamic vinegar

½ teaspoon salt

pinch of dried oregano or thyme (optional)

Cut the broccoli into bite-sized florets (6 to 7 cups). Cook the broccoli florets, either
directly in boiling water or in a steamer basket, until tender. Set aside to cool.

Cut the tomatoes into wedges. (If they aren't juicy summer tomatoes, sprinkle lightly with
salt.) In a small bowl, whisk together the oil, vinegar, salt, and herbs.

In a serving bowl, toss the broccoli and tomatoes with the dressing.

serving & menu ideas ∾

Serve next to Pasta with Caramelized Onions & Blue Cheese (page 27) or Mussels with
Sherry & Saffron (page 168). Or to make a meal of the salad, pile the broccoli on salad
greens, arrange the tomatoes around the edge, and add as many extras as you like: olives,
sweet onion rings, grated feta, ricotta salata or Parmesan cheese, and toasted pine nuts,
almonds, walnuts, or pecans. Drizzle with the dressing and have fresh bread on the side.

tomatoes & onions with mint

This salad goes with almost any dish. Make it when tomatoes are at their peak.

SERVES 4

TIME: 20 MINUTES

(INCLUDES MAKING
VINAIGRETTE AND
CUMIN SALT)

Versatile Vinaigrette (page 222)

Cumin Salt (page 241)

2 large tomatoes

1 small red onion

¼ cup chopped fresh mint

If you don't have any on hand, make the Versatile Vinaigrette and the Cumin Salt.

Remove the core from each tomato and cut the tomatoes in half from stem end to blossom end. Cut each half into thin slices and place on individual plates. Peel the onion and cut it in half. Cut into very thin slices and place on top of the tomato slices.

Drizzle Versatile Vinaigrette over each salad and top with a sprinkling of Cumin Salt and chopped mint.

serving & menu ideas ∾

We especially love this dish with Pine Nut–Crusted Fish (page 161), Lemon Herb Tofu (page 68), and Vietnamese Noodle Salad (page 111).

baby greens with pecans & pears ❧

A perfect balance of flavors and textures, this salad is sure to become a favorite first course to enjoy while supper cooks. Replace the pecans with Sweet Spiced Nuts (page 261) for a special touch.

SERVES 4

TIME: 20 MINUTES

8 cups baby greens or torn romaine or leaf lettuce
   (about 8 ounces)
2 firm but ripe pears
Toasted Pecan Vinaigrette or Versatile Vinaigrette (page 222)
½ cup shredded Parmesan cheese
½ cup toasted pecans

Rinse and dry the salad greens. Cut the pears in half, core them, and cut into matchsticks or thin slices. Lightly coat the pears with a little dressing to prevent discoloration.

In a large salad bowl, toss together the greens and pears. Sprinkle the top with cheese and pecans. Pass the vinaigrette at the table.

INGREDIENT NOTES You can purchase grated cheese, but Parmesan looks and tastes even better if you buy it in a chunk and use a coarse grater to shred it or a sharp vegetable peeler to make curls.

This salad is also good with blue cheese or chèvre.

serving & menu ideas ❧

Perfect with Creamy Lemon Pasta (page 18) or Baked Stuffed Tomatoes (page 49).

corn & pepper salad ∿

SERVES 6

TIME: 25 MINUTES

DRESSING

¼ cup lime juice

3 tablespoons olive oil

2 tablespoons minced fresh cilantro

2 garlic cloves, minced or pressed

dash of Tabasco or other hot pepper sauce

¼ teaspoon salt

1 15-ounce can of corn kernels, drained

1 cup sliced red radishes

1 red bell pepper, diced

1 cup thinly sliced celery

In a serving bowl, whisk together all of the dressing ingredients. Add the corn, radishes, bell peppers, and celery to the bowl. Toss well. Serve at room temperature or chilled.

serving & menu ideas ∿

Prepare this festive salad with Nachos Grandes (page 63) or Bean & Cheese Quesadillas (page 141). Serve it with bread and cheese or hard-boiled eggs, and you have a light meal.

broccoli slaw ∽

What an effortless way to add a nutritious side dish to almost any supper. Make up the whole package of slaw mix and snack on the leftovers—the slaw improves with time.

SERVES 4 TO 6

TIME: 10 MINUTES

3 cups packaged broccoli slaw mix (6 ounces)
1 tablespoon olive oil
1 tablespoon lemon juice, lime juice, or vinegar
salt and pepper

Toss together the broccoli slaw, olive oil, and lemon juice. Add salt and pepper to taste. Serve right away, or to allow the flavors to deepen, let sit at room temperature for 20 minutes or more.

INGREDIENT NOTE Broccoli slaw mixes can be found in the produce section of large supermarkets. We like Mann's brand, which includes broccoli, red cabbage, and carrots.

variations ∽

Add chopped raisins, thinly sliced red onions or scallions, chopped cilantro, sliced or chopped celery, grated carrots, and/or sliced or minced red bell peppers.

For creaminess, add a tablespoon of mayonnaise.

serving & menu ideas ∽

This is a nicely textured salad to serve with Bean & Cheese Quesadillas (page 141), Tortilla Melt (page 144), or Savory Bread & Cheese Bake (page 83).

beet salad ∾

Raw beets give this salad a definite earthiness. For a mellower flavor, use cooked beets. Either way, it's a beautiful salad that adds color to your supper.

SERVES 4 TO 6

TIME: 10 TO 15 MINUTES

3 or 4 raw beets
2 tablespoons vinegar
1 tablespoon olive oil
2 teaspoons Dijon mustard
¼ teaspoon salt
2 scallions, minced
2 tablespoons minced fresh parsley
1 teaspoon sugar (optional)

Peel the beets and cut them in half. Place the beets in the bowl of a food processor and pulse a few times until they are reduced to little chunks, or shred the beets with a food processor or by hand using the largest holes of a grater. (You'll need 2½ to 3 cups.)

In a serving bowl, whisk together the vinegar, oil, mustard, and salt. Add the beets, scallions, and parsley and toss well. Add sugar to taste. Serve at room temperature or chilled.

INGREDIENT NOTE To make this salad with cooked beets, use two 15-ounce cans of whole beets, or enough to make about 2 cups shredded.

serving & menu ideas ∾

A quick and easy side dish for pastas, sandwiches, or fish. We especially like it with Green & White Bean Gratin (page 57) and Kasha & Orzo with Portabellas (page 100). For a great combination that's one of our favorite simple suppers, serve Beet Salad and Bean & Walnut Spread (page 255) with rye bread or crackers and a mild cheese and/or hard-boiled eggs.

greek salad

This simple salad goes with many dishes. Or add some or all of the extras we suggest and make a meal of it.

SERVES 2 TO 4

TIME: 15 MINUTES

4 cups sliced romaine lettuce

1 cucumber, peeled and sliced

2 tomatoes, cut into wedges

$1/2$ red or Vidalia onion, thinly sliced

about 12 kalamata olives

$1/2$ cup crumbled feta cheese

DRESSING

$1/3$ cup olive oil (extra-virgin is nice)

3 tablespoons red wine vinegar

$1/2$ teaspoon salt

$1/4$ teaspoon dried oregano

pinch of black pepper

Fill a serving bowl or platter with the romaine. Arrange the cucumbers, tomatoes, onion, olives, and feta on top. Whisk together the dressing ingredients and pour over the salad.

serving & menu ideas ‿

Instead of making the dressing, just sprinkle the oregano directly on the salad and have cruets of olive oil and vinegar and salt-and-pepper shakers on the table. This is a great side salad for Greek Frittata (page 78), Seared Scallops (page 169), or Pine Nut–Crusted Fish (page 161). To transform it into a satisfying one-dish meal, add stuffed grape leaves, chickpeas or butter beans, and/or artichoke hearts. Or serve with Herbed Hummus (page 253) and warm pita bread.

pan-asian slaw

We call this Pan-Asian Slaw because the hot oil technique is used all over Asia. The hot oil intensifies and yet mellows the flavor of the scallions.

SERVES 4

TIME: 10 MINUTES

6 ounces Asian slaw mix (about 3 cups)

⅓ cup thinly sliced scallions

1 tablespoon vegetable oil

¼ teaspoon salt

1 teaspoon sugar

1½ tablespoons rice vinegar or white vinegar

Place the slaw in a serving bowl. Put the scallions on top, but do not stir.

In a small microwave-safe cup or in a small pan, heat the oil until hot—almost smoking—and pour it over the scallions. Sprinkle on the salt, sugar, and vinegar and toss well. Serve right away or keep refrigerated for up to a few days.

INGREDIENT NOTE If your store doesn't have Asian slaw mix (shredded napa cabbage, celery, and carrots), make this recipe with a regular slaw mix.

serving & menu ideas ∾

Try this slaw alongside Sichuan Silken Tofu (page 72), Oven-Roasted Miso Sesame Salmon (page 155), or noodles tossed with Spicy Peanut Sauce (page 256).

fresh tomato & mozzarella salad ∾

*We make this summer salad from the beginning to the end of
tomato season, and we love it every time. It's beautiful
made with heirloom tomatoes of different colors.*

SERVES 4 TO 6

TIME: 15 MINUTES

2 pounds tomatoes

12 ounces fresh mozzarella

¼ cup chopped fresh basil

¼ cup olive oil (extra-virgin is nice)

½ teaspoon salt

black pepper

Cut the tomatoes into ½-inch dice (about 4 cups). Cut the mozzarella into ½-inch dice
(about 1½ cups). Put them in a large serving bowl. Add the basil. Stir in the olive oil and
the salt. Add pepper to taste. Serve at room temperature.

variations ∾

Try feta cheese (about 1 cup crumbled) instead of mozzarella.

Artichoke hearts, pine nuts, olives, and minced red peppers are all delicious in the
salad.

Toss Fresh Tomato & Mozzarella Salad with hot pasta—the basil will become more
fragrant and the mozzarella will begin to melt.

serving & menu ideas ∾

Just right with Fettuccine with Fresh Herbs (page 24). Or pile it on toasted bread for crostini. For a summer buffet, serve it with Potato Salad with Green & White Beans (page 105),
Corn on the Cob (page 188), and a platter of melon wedges.

wilted spinach salad
with pecans & asiago ∾

SERVES 4

TIME: 15 MINUTES

10 ounces fresh baby spinach (about 10 cups, loosely packed)

1 tablespoon olive oil

2 garlic cloves, thinly sliced

¼ cup raisins or currants

1 cup toasted pecans

½ cup finely grated Asiago or Parmesan cheese (about 1 ounce)

salt and pepper

lemon wedges

Rinse and drain the spinach. Heat the oil in a skillet or saucepan and cook the garlic for a few seconds, until sizzling. Add as much spinach as the pan will hold and cook, stirring often. As the spinach wilts, keep adding more until it is all in the pan. Cook until just wilted but still bright green.

Put the spinach in a serving bowl or on individual plates and top with raisins, pecans, and grated cheese. Sprinkle with salt and pepper. Serve with lemon wedges.

serving & menu ideas ∾

We also love this dish drizzled with Toasted Pecan Vinaigrette (page 222). It's a fine side dish for Creamy Lemon Pasta (page 18), Summer Panzanella (page 108), or Lemony Couscous with Chickpeas (page 97).

chipotle potato salad ◞

Here's a potato salad with a spicy twist. It's perfect for a picnic on a hot day or for supper on a chilly evening.

SERVES 4 TO 6

TIME: 30 MINUTES

6 cups diced potatoes (1-inch cubes)
1 teaspoon salt
2 celery stalks
2 scallions
1 bell pepper, preferably red or yellow
Chipotle Mayonnaise (page 223)

Place the potatoes in a saucepan with enough water to cover. Add the salt, cover, and bring to a boil. Reduce the heat and simmer until the potatoes are tender, 10 to 15 minutes.

While the potatoes cook, finely chop the celery and scallions. Cut the pepper into small pieces. Put the chopped vegetables into a serving bowl.

When the potatoes are done, drain them in a colander and run cold water over them to cool. Add the potatoes to the bowl with the other vegetables, add the Chipotle Mayonnaise, and toss well. Add salt to taste. Serve at room temperature or chilled.

serving & menu ideas ◞

Garnish with cherry tomatoes, cilantro, or Spanish olives. Serve with Corn on the Cob (page 188) and Broccoli Slaw (page 208) in summer. In winter, good with Tomato Tortilla Soup (page 117).

carrot salad with raspberry vinaigrette ∾

We rely on this little carrot salad over and over to add color, sweetness, and crunch to many meals. It's even prettier topped with fresh raspberries. (See photo on page 202.)

SERVES 4

TIME: 10 MINUTES

1 to 2 tablespoons raspberry wine vinegar
2 teaspoons sugar
½ teaspoon salt
1 tablespoon vegetable oil
3 or 4 carrots
¼ cup chopped fresh parsley

In a bowl, whisk together the vinegar, sugar, salt, and oil. Peel and grate the carrots (to make about 2 cups). Add the carrots and the parsley to the bowl and mix well.

Serve at room temperature or chilled. The salad will keep for a day or two in the refrigerator, but use the smaller amount of vinegar if you plan to make it ahead because the vinegar flavor may become sharper as it sits. You can always add more vinegar right before serving.

serving & menu ideas ∾

Try this salad next to Moroccan Spiced Fish (page 157), Spinach Cheese Burritos (page 146), Green & White Bean Gratin (page 57), one of the risottos (pages 89–92), Seared Scallops (page 169), Pasta with Olives Piquant (page 19), Pasta with Greens & Ricotta (page 21), Red Lentil Soup with Greens (page 121) . . . we could go on and on.

Caesar Salad with Caesar Dressing (page 109)

**dressings,
condiments &
seasonings**

caesar dressing ∾

This is the classic dressing for romaine lettuce, but it is delicious on any tossed salad. Drizzle it on steamed vegetables for something special.

YIELDS ½ CUP

TIME: 5 MINUTES

2 tablespoons red wine vinegar or cider vinegar
2 tablespoons mayonnaise
½ teaspoon Dijon mustard
1 teaspoon soy sauce or Worcestershire sauce
¼ cup grated Parmesan or Pecorino Romano cheese
½ teaspoon salt
pinch of black pepper
½ cup olive oil

Whisk together all of the ingredients.

Store leftovers in the refrigerator for up to a week.

variation ∾

To make vegan Caesar Dressing, use an eggless mayonnaise, sometimes called Nayonnaise. Nayonnaise and vegetarian Worcestershire sauce are available in natural foods stores and large supermarkets.

russian dressing ∾

Homemade Russian Dressing can be made in minutes from stuff you probably have on hand, and its flavor is fresher and brighter than bottled.

YIELDS 1 SCANT CUP

TIME: 5 MINUTES

$^1\!/_2$ cup mayonnaise

$^1\!/_4$ cup ketchup

2 teaspoons white or cider vinegar or 1 tablespoon lemon juice

pinch of black pepper

ADD ANY OR ALL:

∾ 1 tablespoon minced scallions or red onions

∾ 2 tablespoons minced tomatoes

∾ $^1\!/_2$ teaspoon dried dill (1$^1\!/_2$ teaspoons fresh)

∾ 2 teaspoons prepared horseradish

∾ 1 tablespoon minced pickles or relish (sour, sweet, or dill)

In a small bowl, combine all of the ingredients.

Plain Russian Dressing will keep in the refrigerator for several weeks. If you add scallions, red onions, or fresh tomatoes, it will keep for 3 or 4 days.

versatile vinaigrette ♋

*A basic vinaigrette can be quickly made with only a few key
ingredients found in the pantry.*

YIELDS 1⅓ CUPS

TIME: 5 TO 10 MINUTES

⅓ cup vinegar or lemon juice

½ teaspoon salt

1 teaspoon Dijon mustard

1 garlic clove, pressed

¼ teaspoon black pepper

1 cup olive oil (extra-virgin is nice)

Either whisk together all of the ingredients or whirl them in a blender for a few seconds.

Vinaigrette will keep in the refrigerator for weeks. When cold, the oil tends to become
milky-looking, partially solidified, so remove the dressing from the refrigerator and let it
sit at room temperature for 15 to 20 minutes before serving.

variations ♋

HERBED VINAIGRETTE

Add fresh or dried herbs. Whisk in 1 to 2 tablespoons of minced fresh dill, chives, tarragon,
thyme, basil, mint, or marjoram, or ½ to 1 teaspoon of dried. For the best flavor, allow dried
herbs to steep in the vinaigrette for at least half
an hour.

TOASTED PECAN VINAIGRETTE

Add 2 tablespoons of toasted pecans. Purée all of
the ingredients in a blender for about 30 seconds,
until smooth and thick. (In this vinaigrette, we
especially like balsamic vinegar or red or white
wine vinegar.)

Baby Greens with Pecans & Pears (page 206)

sour cream lemon dressing ∾

*We hope you have a microplane grater (see page 290), because
the quality of the lemon zest makes a big difference.*

YIELDS ¾ CUP

TIME: 10 MINUTES

1 tablespoon grated lemon peel

¼ cup lemon juice

¼ cup olive oil

¼ cup sour cream

½ teaspoon salt

In a small bowl, whisk the ingredients until smooth and creamy.

Keeps in the refrigerator for a week or more.

chipotle mayonnaise ∾

¾ cup mayonnaise

2 tablespoons minced canned chipotles in adobo sauce
  (see page 286)

YIELDS 1 CUP

TIME: 5 MINUTES

2 tablespoons lime or lemon juice

Whisk together the ingredients. Keeps in the refrigerator for at least 2 weeks.

serving ideas ∾

Spread the mayonnaise on a baguette with roasted vegetables, baby greens, and sliced
Cheddar. Put a dollop on poached fish or steamed vegetables. Serve as a dip for roasted
potatoes. Or use as a dressing for pasta, vegetable, or potato salads.

herbed aioli ❧

Take a few minutes to turn mayonnaise into something special. Aioli is a flavorful topping for steamed vegetables of all types, potatoes, hard-boiled eggs, fish, and shrimp, as well as a dressing for a simple salad, a dip for artichokes—even a sandwich spread.

YIELDS ⅔ CUP

TIME: 5 MINUTES

½ cup mayonnaise

1 or 2 tablespoons olive oil (extra-virgin is nice)

1 garlic clove, pressed

1 tablespoon lemon juice

1 tablespoon minced fresh dill or tarragon (1 teaspoon dried dill)

1 tablespoon minced parsley and/or scallions (optional)

dash of black pepper

Whisk together the ingredients in a small bowl. Keep refrigerated.

variation ❧

SAFFRON AIOLI

Prepare aioli, omitting the herbs. In a cup, crumble a pinch of saffron into a tablespoon of hot water and set aside for a few minutes. Crush the saffron with the back of a spoon to infuse the water with the saffron flavor. Stir the saffron water into the aioli. As it sits, the saffron will continue to bleed into the aioli, so stir before serving.

cilantro lime dressing ∾

The clean, fresh flavors of cilantro and lime make this one of our all-time favorite dressings. If you like a smooth, emulsified dressing, make it in a blender.

YIELDS ¾ CUP

TIME: 10 MINUTES

¼ cup chopped fresh cilantro

1 or 2 thinly sliced scallions

¼ cup lime juice

¼ teaspoon salt

½ teaspoon red pepper flakes (optional)

¼ cup olive oil

Whisk together all of the ingredients in a bowl. Or for a bright green, smooth dressing, in a blender on low speed, whirl the cilantro, scallions, lime juice, salt, and red pepper flakes, if using, until smooth. Add the olive oil in a steady stream and as soon as the dressing is thick, turn off the blender.

Store in the refrigerator for up to a week.

serving ideas ∾

Adds a wonderful flavor to rice, potato, or bean salads, such as Southwestern Black Bean Salad (page 104). Delicious drizzled on avocado cubes or shredded jicama. Excellent as a dressing for fish or shrimp.

cocktail sauce ᔰ

*Who knew that putting together a robust little cocktail sauce was
so easy? Plus it doesn't have the corn syrup and flavor
enhancers of commercially prepared sauce.*

YIELDS ¾ CUP

TIME: 5 MINUTES

½ cup ketchup
¼ cup prepared horseradish
2 teaspoons lemon juice

In a small bowl, combine the ingredients.

Keeps in the refrigerator for 2 to 3 weeks.

tartar sauce ᔰ

*Easy to put together in a couple of minutes and much fresher-
tasting than commercial products. Makes a familiar topping
for fish and other seafood and a great sandwich spread.*

YIELDS ¾ CUP

TIME: 5 MINUTES

½ cup mayonnaise
¼ cup pickle relish
2 teaspoons lemon juice

In a small bowl, stir together the mayonnaise, relish, and lemon juice.

Will keep in the refrigerator for a couple of weeks.

INGREDIENT NOTE For the relish, substitute ¼ cup finely chopped sweet or dill pickles, an
additional teaspoon of lemon juice, and a teaspoon of sugar if you wish.

variations ᔰ

For extra flavor, add a tablespoon of minced scallions or red onions, a tablespoon of
minced capers, a teaspoon of minced fresh dill or tarragon, or a few drops of Tabasco or
other hot pepper sauce.

Po' Boy Sandwich (page 172)

duck sauce

Once you've made this easy Duck Sauce, you'll never go back to store-bought!

YIELDS ¾ CUP

TIME: 5 MINUTES

²/₃ cup peach or apricot preserves
2 tablespoons white or cider vinegar
4 teaspoons soy sauce

Mix all of the ingredients together in a small bowl.

Store in the refrigerator; it will keep for at least a month.

serving ideas

Serve this as a dipping sauce for Easy Egg Rolls (page 148) or any time you need a little sweet-and-sour jolt on a stir-fry or sauté.

barbecue sauce

Easy, no-fuss sauce for your favorite barbecue.

YIELDS ¾ CUP

TIME: 5 MINUTES

²/₃ cup ketchup
1 tablespoon soy sauce
1 tablespoon Dijon or yellow mustard
2 teaspoons white or cider vinegar
2 teaspoons brown sugar or honey
1 to 3 teaspoons Tabasco or other hot pepper sauce, chili paste, or adobo sauce from chipotles (see page 286)

In a small bowl, whisk together all of the ingredients.

Store in the refrigerator; it will keep for at least a month.

pineapple chutney ∾

*This colorful chutney, better than any you can buy in a jar, adds
a sweet-and-sour note to curries, baked tofu, or any spicy dish
and can even put a new spin on that same old peanut
butter sandwich.*

YIELDS 1½ CUPS

TIME: 20 MINUTES

1 20-ounce can of pineapple chunks in juice
2 teaspoons vegetable oil
½ teaspoon black mustard seeds
1½ teaspoons grated peeled ginger root
¼ cup raisins
2 tablespoons sugar
2 tablespoons cider vinegar
pinch of salt

Drain the pineapple, reserving the juice. Chop the pineapple chunks a bit.

In a saucepan, heat the oil until hot but not smoking. Add the mustard seeds, and when
they begin to pop (almost immediately), add the ginger. Cook for half a minute and then
stir in the pineapple and ¼ cup of the juice. Add the raisins, sugar, vinegar, and salt and
bring to a simmer. Reduce the heat and cook uncovered at a low simmer, stirring occasionally, until most of the liquid is evaporated, about 15 minutes.

Serve hot, at room temperature, or chilled. The chutney will keep in the refrigerator for
up to 3 weeks.

INGREDIENT NOTES You can substitute fennel seeds for the mustard seeds and dried cranberries for the raisins.

serving ideas ∾

This chutney adds something special to Roasted Vegetable Curry (page 53) and Spicy
Potatoes & Spinach (page 45).

Curried Cauliflower & Chickpea Soup (page 120)

cranberry chutney ∾

Crimson red with a bright fruit flavor, this chutney is a great condiment for all curries.

YIELDS 2 CUPS

TIME: 25 MINUTES

1 tablespoon vegetable oil
2 cups chopped onions
½ teaspoon salt
⅛ teaspoon black pepper
1 tablespoon white or cider vinegar
1 tablespoon grated peeled ginger root
1 teaspoon grated lemon or orange peel
pinch of cayenne
1 16-ounce can of whole-berry cranberry sauce

In a saucepan on medium-high heat, warm the oil and cook the onions, salt, and pepper, until the onions are translucent, about 5 minutes. Add the vinegar, ginger, citrus peel, and cayenne and simmer for 10 minutes, stirring occasionally. Add the cranberry sauce and stir well.

Serve warm, at room temperature, or chilled. The chutney will keep in the refrigerator for at least a month.

serving ideas ∾

A dollop of Cranberry Chutney makes Curried Cauliflower & Chickpea Soup (page 120) absolutely delicious. Try a dollop on Baked Acorn Squash Crescents (page 198) or Roasted Sweet Potatoes (page 197), or next to Indian Potato Salad with Cilantro Omelet (page 106).

cilantro yogurt sauce ∾

Refreshing and pretty, this sauce makes a tangy and colorful garnish for curries, stews, and soups.

YIELDS 2 CUPS

TIME: 5 MINUTES

2 cups plain yogurt
$1/3$ cup chopped fresh cilantro
$1/2$ teaspoon sugar (optional)
$1/4$ teaspoon salt

In a blender, purée $1/2$ cup of the yogurt with the cilantro, sugar, and salt until smooth and bright green. Fold the cilantro-yogurt mixture into the remaining yogurt. If you prefer, mix together all of the ingredients in a bowl. It won't be as green, but it will taste just fine.

serving ideas ∾

Serve with Navajo Stew (page 46), West Indian Red Beans & Coconut Rice (page 69), or Curried Cauliflower & Chickpea Soup (page 120).

quick avocado & corn salsa ❧

Spruce up your favorite homemade or store-bought salsa.

YIELDS 2 CUPS

TIME: 10 MINUTES

1 cup of your favorite salsa

1 cup frozen corn kernels, thawed

¼ cup chopped fresh cilantro (optional)

1 ripe avocado

1 teaspoon lime or lemon juice (optional)

Place the salsa, corn, and cilantro in a bowl. Slice the avocado in half lengthwise and remove the pit. Cut the avocado flesh into cubes in the shell by making crosshatch slices about ½ inch apart. With a spoon, scoop out the avocado cubes into the bowl with the salsa and corn. Mix well. Add lime or lemon juice and salt to taste.

INGREDIENT NOTES There are several methods for thawing frozen corn: Zap for a minute in a microwave oven, immerse in hot water (and then drain), let sit at room temperature for an hour or so, or thaw in the refrigerator overnight.

For extra-fresh flavor or to stretch the quantity, add a chopped ripe tomato.

serving ideas ❧

Use as a topping for Black Beans with Pickled Red Onions (page 58) in place of the pickled onions, or as a colorful side for Chipotle Scrambled Eggs (page 84) or Chipotle Potato Salad (page 216).

roasted garlic ∽

*Roasting mellows and sweetens the pungent flavor of raw garlic.
Roasted garlic is useful for enhancing salad dressings, sauces,
soups, and stews, and it can be used as a spread on bread
all by itself.*

HANDS-ON TIME: 10 MINUTES

OVEN TIME: 40 MINUTES

large heads of garlic

olive oil or vegetable oil

Preheat the oven to 375°.

Remove the outer papery skin of each head of garlic, but keep the cloves connected. Cut off the top, about ½ inch of the stem end, so that the tips of the topmost cloves are cut flat across. Place the heads of garlic in an oiled baking dish and cover with foil.

Bake until the cloves are soft to the touch, about 40 minutes. Cool.

To use: With gentle pressure from the bottom, the root end, squeeze the softened garlic cloves out of the husks. You can squeeze the roasted garlic out of the whole head or out of separated individual cloves.

Roasted garlic will keep in the refrigerator for about 2 weeks.

serving ideas ∽

Serve warm bread with a small dish of olive oil for dipping and a head of roasted garlic for squeezing. Make Roasted Garlic Butter (page 236). Use in cooking when you want a mellow garlic flavor.

chili powder ∾

Make your own custom-made Chili Powder that reflects your flavor preferences and is free of unwanted ingredients, such as dried garlic and anticaking agents. After you've used this basic blend, adjust the recipe to fit your taste.

YIELDS ⅓ CUP

TIME: 5 MINUTES

1 tablespoon ground cumin

1 tablespoon ground coriander

1 tablespoon dried oregano

1 tablespoon paprika

1½ teaspoons dried thyme

½ teaspoon cayenne

¼ teaspoon ground cloves

1½ teaspoons dried sage (optional)

Mix all of the ingredients together. Store in a well-sealed container.

INGREDIENT NOTE For a fresher and more aromatic Chili Powder, toast whole cumin and coriander seeds and then grind with whole cloves and the rest of the ingredients in a spice grinder.

flavored butter ∽

Flavored butter can make plain food instantly interesting by enlivening it with the flavors of fresh herbs, ginger, citrus, chiles, or roasted garlic. Keep some in the freezer to use in cooking or at the table. Give an instant flavor boost to plain steamed vegetables, broiled or grilled fish, eggs, grains, pasta, corn on the cob, or mashed potatoes. Slather it on fresh bread, rolls, or biscuits.

**YIELDS
GENEROUS ½ CUP**

TIME: 10 MINUTES

½ cup butter, softened

ingredients for one of the flavors listed

Soften the butter at room temperature, or microwave for about 10 seconds. With a flexible spatula, mix in the flavor ingredients. Use the spatula to form the butter into a log on a piece of aluminum foil, plastic wrap, or waxed paper. Wrap the log and close tightly. Refrigerate or freeze.

For the best flavor protection, place the wrapped butter log in a labeled and dated plastic storage bag. Well-wrapped Flavored Butters will keep in the refrigerator for about 2 weeks and in the freezer for 6 months. To use frozen butter, unwrap and slice off as much as you need. It may crumble if cut immediately out of the freezer, but it will slice cleanly after a few minutes at room temperature.

roasted garlic butter ∽
Mild and mellow garlic flavor.

1 head of Roasted Garlic (page 234),
the softened cloves squeezed out of the papery husks

herbed butter ∾

*Fresh herb flavor any time of year. Delicious with just one herb, or mix
and match.*

¼ cup chopped fresh basil, tarragon, dill, or chives

gremolata butter ∾

An Italian classic, fragrant with lemon.

2 tablespoons minced fresh parsley
2 tablespoons lemon juice
1 tablespoon grated lemon peel
1 garlic clove, minced or pressed

chipotle lime butter ∾

Canned chipotle peppers add smoky, spicy heat.

1 tablespoon minced canned chipotles in adobo sauce
   (see page 286)
2 tablespoons lime juice

ginger butter ∾

The bright flavor of ginger, especially good with seafood.

2 tablespoons finely grated peeled ginger root
2 tablespoons chopped fresh chives
a few splashes of Tabasco or other hot pepper sauce
1 tablespoon chopped fresh mint (optional)

curry powder ∾

A fresh curry powder that is mildly hot and packs a flavorful punch compared to commercial blends, which may sit on store shelves for months past their prime. Stir into butter or mayonnaise and use to flavor rice, roasted potatoes, or fish.

YIELDS ½ CUP

TIME: 5 MINUTES

4 tablespoons cumin seeds

1 tablespoon turmeric

1 tablespoon cardamom seeds

½ teaspoon cayenne

½ teaspoon ground cinnamon (optional)

Toast the cumin seeds until aromatic, a couple of minutes, in a hot, dry skillet while stirring or shaking continuously or in a toaster oven. Allow to cool before grinding.

In a spice grinder, whirl all of the spices until finely ground. Allow the spice grinder to sit for a minute before removing the cover to avoid the discomfort of cayenne dust in your eyes and nose. Store Curry Powder in a tightly covered jar in the cupboard.

moroccan spice mix ∾

We use this aromatic spice mix to flavor roasted vegetables and baked or grilled shrimp or fish.

YIELDS ⅓ CUP

TIME: 5 MINUTES

2 tablespoons ground cumin

2 teaspoons ground ginger or cinnamon

2 teaspoons paprika

2 teaspoons turmeric

½ teaspoon cayenne or black pepper

1 teaspoon salt

Stir together all of the ingredients. Store in a well-sealed container in the cupboard.

serving ideas ∾

Sprinkle Moroccan Spice Mix on Roasted Sweet Potatoes (page 197) before putting them in the oven. Make a variation of Old Bay Roasted Fish & Vegetables (page 164) by using Moroccan in place of Old Bay seasonings. Stir ½ teaspoon of Moroccan Spice Mix into ½ cup of yogurt for a flavorful little sauce.

salt & pepper

Salt and pepper are sometimes the only seasonings you need to bring out the flavor of simple dishes and fresh ingredients.

∾ **Salt** may be the single most important ingredient in the kitchen because it enhances the flavors of all other foods, even sweets. The kinds of salt commonly available differ in taste, texture, and makeup.

TABLE SALT, mined from the earth, can be so highly refined that it loses character. Processing removes the iodine naturally present in salt and added anticaking agents can leave an aftertaste.

IODIZED SALT contains iodine, added to replace what was lost in the refining process.

SEA SALT has a brighter, more complex flavor and retains beneficial minerals, including iodine. It is available either coarse or fine-grained.

KOSHER SALT, which has no additives, is less intensely flavored than sea salt or table salt, and it dissolves quickly. Its coarse crystals don't fit through the holes of a standard salt shaker, so keep it in a small covered dish next to the stove and on the table.

If you have the opportunity, sample the unusual salts found in many natural foods stores and gourmet specialty shops, such as crystalline, mild *fleur de sel*—a large-grained gray salt from France's northern coast—black lava and red clay salts from Hawaii, Peruvian pink salt, English Maldon sea salt, and smoked Danish salt.

∾ **Pepper** is the other seasoning we take for granted but would dearly miss if we had to do without. Because their volatile oils are released after being crushed or ground, peppercorns quickly lose flavor and aroma. So instead of packaged ground pepper, we prefer to use whole peppercorns and grind them with a peppermill, spice grinder, or mortar and pestle. The flavor of freshly ground pepper is warm, intense, and complex.

Green, black, and white pepper look and taste quite different from one another. They all come from berries of the same tropical plant, but they're harvested at different stages.

GREEN PEPPERCORNS are harvested when they're unripe, soft, and aromatic. Green pepper can be sprinkled directly onto food or first mashed into a paste.

BLACK PEPPERCORNS are picked green and then turn black when dried. Black pepper has a more complex, hotter, sweeter taste than green.

WHITE PEPPERCORNS are picked when fully ripened, soaked to remove their red outer skins, and then dried. White pepper has a mild flavor and is used in creamed soups and sauces where its color is preferable.

cumin salt ✏

Cumin salt is a handy seasoning for all sorts of dishes. Crisp crudités are delicious dipped into it, or you can use it to season as you would plain salt. Sprinkle into scrambled eggs or on plain rice, potatoes, fish, corn on the cob, or sliced fresh vegetables, such as tomatoes and cucumbers.

YIELDS ¼ CUP

TIME: 5 MINUTES

2 tablespoons cumin seeds

2 tablespoons salt

Toast the cumin seeds until aromatic, a couple of minutes, in a toaster oven or in a hot, dry skillet while stirring or shaking continuously. Allow to cool before grinding.

Grind the cooled, toasted cumin seeds and the salt in a spice grinder.

Store at room temperature, tightly covered.

Red Pepper Butter Sauce (page 247)

sauces & spreads

blender tomato hot sauce ❧

This is the hot sauce we make regularly at the restaurant to ladle over burritos, enchiladas, tostadas, casseroles, and stuffed vegetables. Cooking the onions and peppers quickly on high heat brings out flavor with less simmering time.

YIELDS 2 CUPS

TIME: 20 MINUTES

1 tablespoon vegetable oil or olive oil

1 medium onion, coarsely chopped

1 small or ½ large bell pepper, chopped

1 teaspoon ground cumin

1 teaspoon ground coriander

¼ teaspoon cayenne or ½ teaspoon red pepper flakes

1 15-ounce can of tomatoes

¼ cup chopped fresh cilantro (optional)

In a heavy saucepan or skillet, heat the oil until it is almost smoking. Stir in the onion and bell peppers and sprinkle with salt. Cook on high heat, stirring often, until the peppers are blistered and beginning to brown, about 4 minutes. Stir in the cumin, coriander, and cayenne or red pepper flakes and remove from the heat.

In a blender, purée the cooked onions and peppers with the tomatoes. Return the sauce to the pan, add the cilantro, and salt to taste. Simmer uncovered for about 10 minutes, stirring occasionally. (If the simmering sauce splatters, partially cover the pan.)

This sauce will keep in the refrigerator for at least 2 weeks.

INGREDIENT NOTES If you use red bell pepper, the sauce will be a brighter red.

Substitute a fresh chile, seeded for a milder "hot," for the cayenne; cook it with the onion. For a smoky flavor, use 1 or 2 tablespoons of canned chipotles in adobo sauce (see page 286) in place of cayenne.

serving & menu ideas ❧

Simmer vegetables such as onions, peppers, and zucchini in the sauce and serve over cornbread. Try it on Mexican Polenta-Stuffed Peppers (page 94) or to cook the eggs in Poached Huevos Rancheros (page 79).

creamy caper sauce ∾

*A rendition of creamy white sauce—capers, herbs, and lemon
make it different.*

YIELDS 2 CUPS

TIME: 20 MINUTES

¼ cup butter
¼ cup unbleached white flour
2½ cups hot milk
⅓ cup dry white wine (optional)
2 tablespoons drained capers
½ teaspoon dried tarragon or dill
¼ teaspoon salt
⅛ teaspoon black pepper
1 tablespoon lemon juice

In a heavy saucepan on low heat, melt the butter. Whisk in the flour and cook for a
couple of minutes, stirring constantly. Whisk in the hot milk, adding it in a slow, steady
stream. Cook, stirring often, until the sauce is thickened, 4 to 5 minutes.

Stir in the wine, capers, tarragon or dill, salt, and pepper and continue to cook for
5 minutes.

Stir in the lemon juice and add more salt and pepper to taste. (If you don't add the wine,
you may need to add a little extra milk.)

serving & menu ideas ∾

This sauce is delicious on fish. Try it on pasta, too; it's especially pretty on spinach fettuccine topped with chopped tomatoes and grated Parmesan cheese. We sometimes add
chunks of cooked salmon or steamed broccoli or cauliflower florets as well. Make extra
to ladle on your favorite vegetable on a bed of couscous, rice, or noodles.

sauce niçoise ❧

This pungent, quickly cooked sauce studded with olives and capers imparts the zesty flavors of southern France.

YIELDS 2 CUPS

TIME: 15 MINUTES

1 cup finely chopped tomatoes
½ cup chopped pitted kalamata olives
¼ cup chopped fresh parsley
2 tablespoons capers, drained
2 tablespoons lemon juice
black pepper
1 tablespoon extra-virgin olive oil
2 garlic cloves, minced or pressed
½ teaspoon dried thyme

In a bowl, mix together the tomatoes, olives, parsley, capers, and lemon juice. Sprinkle generously with black pepper.

Warm the oil in a saucepan on low heat, add the garlic and thyme, and cook for a minute. Add the tomato mixture, increase the heat to medium-high, and simmer, stirring frequently, just until the tomatoes soften and become saucy, about 5 minutes.

INGREDIENT NOTE Dried thyme varies in freshness and potency, so use more or less depending on the strength and flavor of yours. If you have fresh thyme, use about 2 teaspoons.

serving & menu ideas ❧

Grill, broil, pan-fry, or poach your favorite fish (see page 152), and top it with Sauce Niçoise. It's also good on shrimp or scallops. Stir some into Potato Salad with Green & White Beans (page 105) to transform it into a fresh new dish.

red pepper butter sauce ∽

*This beautiful sunset-red sauce with flecks of green herbs
turns pasta, vegetables, potatoes, or fish into a work of art.
Leftover sauce keeps in the refrigerator for a week or two.*

YIELDS 1½ CUPS

TIME: 10 MINUTES

½ cup olive oil

6 garlic cloves

½ cup butter, at room temperature

1 cup canned roasted red peppers (more or less is fine)

1 tablespoon lemon juice

½ teaspoon salt

2 tablespoons chopped fresh dill or basil (optional)

In a small skillet on medium heat, warm the olive oil. Add the garlic cloves and cook for about 3 minutes, until the garlic is golden. Remove from the heat.

In a blender on medium speed, purée the butter, roasted red peppers, lemon juice, and salt. Pour in the oil and garlic and whirl until smooth. Taste and add more lemon juice or salt if needed. If using dill or basil, stir it in by hand.

INGREDIENT NOTE To make the sauce with fresh bell peppers, stem, seed, and chop a large red bell pepper or 2 medium ones and cook in the oil with the garlic until soft, 12 to 15 minutes. Whirl in a blender with the butter, lemon juice, and salt until smooth.

serving & menu ideas ∽

This sauce is excellent on pasta, such as penne or shells. For a beautiful color contrast, put 1½ cups of frozen peas in with the cooking pasta a couple of minutes before you drain it. Use the sauce in place of the oil in Pasta with Olives Piquant (page 19). Stir some into polenta or ladle a bit over a side of steamed asparagus or broccoli.

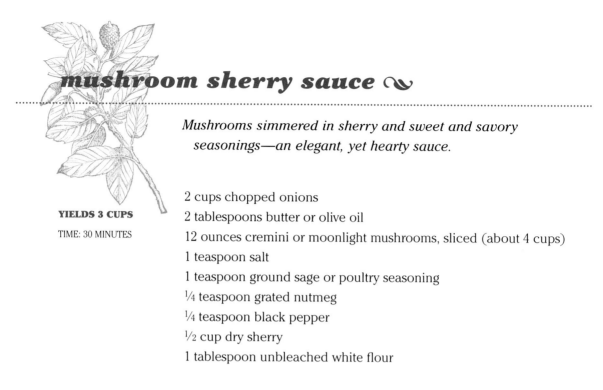

mushroom sherry sauce ∾

Mushrooms simmered in sherry and sweet and savory seasonings—an elegant, yet hearty sauce.

YIELDS 3 CUPS

TIME: 30 MINUTES

2 cups chopped onions

2 tablespoons butter or olive oil

12 ounces cremini or moonlight mushrooms, sliced (about 4 cups)

1 teaspoon salt

1 teaspoon ground sage or poultry seasoning

¼ teaspoon grated nutmeg

¼ teaspoon black pepper

½ cup dry sherry

1 tablespoon unbleached white flour

In a covered saucepan on medium heat, cook the onions in the butter or oil for about 5 minutes, stirring once or twice. Increase the heat and add the mushrooms, salt, sage, nutmeg, and pepper and cook covered for 3 or 4 minutes, until the mushrooms begin to release liquid. Add the sherry and cook uncovered for 5 minutes.

In a cup, combine the flour and ¼ cup of water to make a smooth paste. Whisk the paste into the mushrooms and cook on low heat, stirring constantly, until thickened.

serving & menu ideas ∾

Stir into hot pasta and top with grated cheese. Excellent on fish, rice, and baked or mashed potatoes. This sauce is even hearty enough to serve as a meal over toast points.

brown butter sauce ❧

We developed this little sauce, so easily made, to serve on Seared Scallops (page 169). But it's so good that soon we were drizzling it on plain vegetables, fish, and grains, too.

YIELDS ½ CUP

TIME: 10 MINUTES

½ cup butter
2 teaspoons balsamic vinegar

In a small pan on medium-low heat, melt the butter. Simmer for about 4 minutes until the butter melts and the solids sink to the bottom and very soon after turn brown—the butter will become nut-brown in color. Watch it closely because it can turn from nicely nutty brown to badly scorched in the wink of an eye. Remove from the heat, strain through a small sieve if you like, and stir in the balsamic vinegar.

Brown Butter Sauce keeps in the refrigerator for about 2 weeks, and it reheats nicely in a microwave oven.

simple tomato sauce ∾

YIELDS 3 CUPS

TIME: 15 MINUTES

6 garlic cloves, minced or pressed
1 tablespoon olive oil
1 28-ounce can of plum tomatoes
fresh chopped basil to taste
1/2 teaspoon salt
1/2 teaspoon black pepper

In a saucepan on low heat, cook the garlic in the oil for a couple of minutes, until golden. Stir in the juice from the can of tomatoes.

Squeeze the tomatoes with your hand to crush them or cut them coarsely with a knife or kitchen scissors while they're still in the can. Add them to the garlic with the basil, salt, and pepper, bring to a simmer, and cook on low heat for at least 5 minutes.

variations ∾

∾ Cook about a cup of chopped onions with the garlic.
∾ Before adding the garlic, cook some diced vegetables, such as zucchini, bell peppers, or carrots, in the oil until soft.
∾ Add chopped roasted red peppers.
∾ Add 1/2 teaspoon of oregano or crushed red pepper flakes.
∾ Purée the sauce in a blender until smooth.
∾ Stir about 1/4 cup of cream cheese or sour cream into the sauce just before serving.
∾ Add a couple of tablespoons of capers, sliced olives, and some red pepper flakes for a quick puttanesca sauce.

serving & menu ideas ∾

Ladle over pasta, rice, polenta, broiled fish, breaded and baked eggplant rounds, or even fried eggs on toast. Dress up steamed cauliflower or green beans, or use it as the sauce for Seitan Pizza Subs (page 140).

classic pesto ∾

YIELDS 1 CUP

TIME: 10 MINUTES

⅓ cup toasted pine nuts, almonds, or walnuts, or a mixture

1 garlic clove

2 cups packed fresh basil leaves (about 2½ ounces)

⅓ cup olive oil

¼ teaspoon salt

pinch of black pepper

⅓ cup grated Parmesan cheese (optional)

In the bowl of a food processor, pulse the nuts and garlic until crumbly. Add the basil, oil, salt, pepper, and grated cheese and process until fairly smooth.

variations ∾

Use soy or rice Parmesan for a vegan variation.

If your basil supply is limited, or if you prefer a milder flavor, substitute spinach leaves for up to half of the basil.

Add a touch of lemon juice or some chopped tomatoes.

planning tip ∾

In the summer, when basil is abundant and reasonably priced, make pesto for your freezer. (Multiply this recipe for the amount of basil you have.) Omit the cheese and freeze the mixture in ice cube trays. When they're frozen, pop the cubes out and store in a freezer bag, where they will keep for months. Then, when you're ready for a taste of summer, defrost some cubes and purée with the cheese. The frozen cubes are also handy for tossing into soups, stews, and sauces for a quick flavor boost.

serving & menu ideas ∾

Pasta tossed with pesto and topped with chopped tomatoes is one of our favorite simple suppers. Or stir some pesto into cooked rice or other grains. It also makes a nice sandwich spread—try it on Tortilla Melt (page 144) or a cheese and tomato sandwich. Toss some with leftover pasta and add a few steamed or raw vegetables for a quick pasta salad.

herbed hummus ～

YIELDS 1½ CUPS

TIME: 30 MINUTES

HANDS-ON TIME:
15 MINUTES

CHILLING TIME:
AT LEAST 15 MINUTES

1 15-ounce can of chickpeas, drained
¼ cup tahini
3 tablespoons lemon juice
½ teaspoon salt
1 garlic clove, sliced or chopped
¼ cup chopped fresh parsley
1 tablespoon chopped fresh dill
1 scallion, chopped (optional)

Put the chickpeas, tahini, lemon juice, salt, garlic, and 3 tablespoons of water into the bowl of a food processor. Purée until smooth and creamy, stopping to scrape down the sides of the bowl if necessary. Add the parsley, dill, and scallions. Pulse just until the herbs are integrated; the hummus should be beige with flecks of green rather than a uniform pale green.

Add more lemon juice and salt to taste. Refrigerate for at least 15 minutes so the flavors of the herbs will come through. In a covered container in the refrigerator, Herbed Hummus will keep for 2 or 3 days.

serving & menu ideas ～

Serve with crackers, bread, or crudités. Make into a sandwich with multigrain bread, tomato slices, and lettuce. Serve alongside Greek Salad (page 211) topped with Peppercorn Citrus Marinated Feta (page 201) and include a bowl of Asparagus Avgolemono (page 130) for a Greek-style feast.

sicilian chickpea spread ❧

At Moosewood Restaurant, we're always coming up with new bean spreads. Here's a multipurpose, hummus-like spread, enhanced with rich creamy pine nuts, roasted red peppers, and fresh basil.

YIELDS 2 CUPS

TIME: 15 MINUTES

$\frac{1}{3}$ cup toasted pine nuts

1 15-ounce can of chickpeas, drained

1 large canned roasted red pepper

1 garlic clove

$\frac{1}{4}$ cup olive oil

2 tablespoons lemon juice

$\frac{1}{3}$ cup packed fresh basil leaves

$\frac{1}{4}$ teaspoon salt

generous pinch of black pepper

Place all of the ingredients in the bowl of a food processor and whirl for 2 or 3 minutes, until light and creamy.

serving & menu ideas ❧

For a quick dinner, toss with hot, just-drained pasta and add chopped tomatoes or steamed vegetables. Make extra spread so that you can serve it later with bread or crackers or with vegetable sticks. This spread also makes a great sandwich with lettuce and tomatoes.

bean & walnut spread ↷

This nutty bean purée is inspired by lobio, *a marinated bean salad from the Georgian Republic.*

YIELDS 3 CUPS

TIME: 15 MINUTES

1 cup toasted walnuts

1 28-ounce can of red kidney beans (or 2 15-ounce cans), rinsed
    and drained

2 large garlic cloves, minced or pressed

5 scallions, chopped

2 tablespoons chopped fresh dill

2 tablespoons olive oil

2 tablespoons cider vinegar

$1/2$ teaspoon salt

$1/4$ teaspoon black pepper

In the bowl of a food processor, grind the nuts until they make a smooth paste. Add the beans, garlic, about half of the scallions, the dill, olive oil, vinegar, salt, and pepper and purée until quite smooth.

Serve at room temperature or chilled, in a bowl or on a bed of greens, topped with the remaining scallions. This purée can be kept in the refrigerator for a couple of days. It loses a bit of its tang overnight, so add a little more vinegar to taste.

serving & menu ideas ↷

Some of us love Bean & Walnut Spread as part of a composed salad: Serve it on a bed of greens with hard-boiled eggs, Beet Salad (page 209), creamy Broccoli Slaw (page 208), and rye bread. And it's a fine sandwich spread, with lettuce and tomatoes, or dressed up with roasted red peppers, hard-boiled eggs, or pickles. It's an excellent snack or appetizer with crudités and/or crackers or bread.

spicy peanut sauce ∾

A rich and versatile sauce that can be used to make many delightful suppers. Triple the recipe so you'll have leftovers.

YIELDS ¾ CUP

TIME: 5 MINUTES

⅓ cup peanut butter, smooth or chunky

⅓ cup warm water or apple juice

2 tablespoons soy sauce

1½ tablespoons cider vinegar

½ teaspoon Chinese chili paste or Tabasco or other hot pepper sauce (optional)

1 tablespoon dark sesame oil (optional)

In a small bowl, whisk or stir all of the ingredients until smooth.

variations ∾

PINEAPPLE PEANUT SAUCE

In a saucepan, bring to a simmer a cup of canned crushed pineapple and stir in the Spicy Peanut Sauce ingredients, omitting the water (yields about 1½ cups).

AFRICAN PEANUT SAUCE

In a saucepan, bring a cup of canned diced tomatoes to a simmer and stir in the Spicy Peanut Sauce ingredients, omitting the water and sesame oil (yields about 1½ cups).

SOUTHEAST ASIAN PEANUT SAUCE

Use coconut milk instead of water.

serving & menu ideas ∾

Here are a few ideas to inspire you:

∾ Serve baked fish or tofu on rice with steamed vegetables, such as carrots, broccoli, zucchini, sweet potatoes, cabbage, or snow peas, topped with Spicy Peanut Sauce.

∾ Top a bed of rice with steamed spinach or cabbage, shredded raw carrots, and Spicy Peanut Sauce.

∾ Drizzle warm Spicy Peanut Sauce on a salad of spinach or spring mix topped with cucumbers, celery, and tomatoes.

∾ Dress coleslaw with Pineapple Peanut Sauce for an unusual and delicious side dish.

∾ Stir African Peanut Sauce into white beans, black-eyed peas, or field peas and chopped cooked collards or other greens for a delicious one-pot meal.

∾ Pour Southeast Asian Peanut Sauce over rice noodles or linguine topped with mung bean sprouts and/or cucumber slices. Great with Easy Baked Tofu (page 64).

Cherry Shortbread Crumble (page 265)

desserts

fruit & cheese plates ❧

Perfectly ripe fresh fruit is one the simplest and most enjoyable ways to end a meal. It's effortless, healthful, and satisfying, especially when paired with cheese, its classic partner. Fresh fruit is best when it's in season locally. In fact, when straw-berries finally appear at the farm stand, they're usually our first consideration in planning a menu: What would be a good supper to have before we eat the strawberries?

To create a cheese platter to serve alone or with fruit at the end of a meal, select cheeses with a range of tastes from delicate, mild, and buttery, to strong, rich, and nutty, to salty, sharp, and pungent. Choose a balance of textures from soft and volup-tuous to hard and crumbly. Traditionally, a cheese course moves from mild cheeses to sharp to rich, but for the simplest presentation, arrange cheeses together on a plat-ter with crackers (try crackers seasoned with pepper or rosemary) or thin slices of baguette. A few walnuts and a glass of port might be welcome also.

Some of our favorite ideas for simple fruit and cheese plates are:
- ❧ grapes with Gorgonzola, Brie, or Stilton
- ❧ cherries with nutty Gruyère or Emmental
- ❧ goat cheese with clementines or fresh or dried apricots, dates, or figs
- ❧ feta or ricotta salata with watermelon and cantaloupe
- ❧ pears with Roquefort, Taleggio, or Manchego and toasted walnuts or pine nuts
- ❧ plump dates with aged Parmigiano-Reggiano or with mascarpone and toasted walnuts or almonds
- ❧ a blue cheese surrounded with slices of oranges or Asian pears
- ❧ fresh figs or strawberries with thin wedges of Tuscan Pecorino or Pecorino Romano drizzled with honey and olive oil and sprinkled with freshly ground black pepper
- ❧ In the fall and winter, lots of apple varieties are in season. Choose a couple you're not familiar with and some old favorites. Serve the apples with several cheeses and sample all the different combinations of apples and cheese.

sweet spiced nuts ❧

These glossy, burnished, not-too-sweet and not-too-spicy nuts are irresistible. With fresh or dried fruit, they make an elegant dessert. Or add to one of our Fruit & Cheese Plates. A great little something to snack on, too—we like to keep them around to nibble on when supper is a little late. They keep for up to a month.

YIELDS 3 CUPS

TIME: 25 MINUTES

$^1/_3$ cup sugar

$^1/_2$ teaspoon salt

$^1/_2$ teaspoon black pepper

$^1/_2$ teaspoon ground cardamom

$^1/_2$ teaspoon ground cinnamon

pinch of cayenne (optional)

3 cups shelled nuts (pecans, almonds, walnuts, peanuts, cashews)

Preheat the oven to 350°. Generously oil a baking sheet.

In a saucepan on medium-high heat, stir together the sugar, $^1/_4$ cup of water, salt, pepper, cardamom, cinnamon, and cayenne and bring to a boil. Reduce the heat to a simmer and stir constantly for a minute, until the sugar is dissolved. Remove from the heat and add the nuts and mix well to evenly coat them with the syrup. Remove the coated nuts with a slotted spoon and spread them out on the prepared baking sheet.

Bake until browned, 10 to 15 minutes, stirring once after 5 or 6 minutes. After you've taken them out of the oven, stir again to break apart any clusters. Allow the nuts to cool before serving.

warm plums with mascarpone ∿

Warm caramelized plums are delicious paired with cool and creamy mascarpone. You can also cook the plums under a broiler for about 10 minutes or on a tabletop grill for 5 minutes.

SERVES 4 TO 6

TIME: 25 MINUTES

6 plums

¼ cup packed brown sugar

½ cup mascarpone cheese

1 tablespoon Marsala wine or an orange-flavored liquor, such as Grand Marnier

Preheat the oven to 425°.

Cut the plums in half and remove the pits. Fill each plum cavity with 1 teaspoon of the brown sugar and place the plums in a baking pan. Put 2 tablespoons of water in the bottom of the pan and bake until the plums are browned and somewhat softened, about 20 minutes.

While the plums bake, mix together the mascarpone, Marsala, and the remaining brown sugar. When the plums are done, put a dollop of the mascarpone mixture into each half and serve warm.

caribbean sautéed bananas

Warm, luscious bananas soaked in rum—a little taste of tropical paradise.

SERVES 4

TIME: 20 MINUTES

5 firm bananas

2 tablespoons lime juice

½ cup dark rum

¾ cup packed brown sugar

½ teaspoon ground cinnamon

¼ teaspoon ground ginger

Peel the bananas, cut on the diagonal into thick slices, and place in a large bowl. Sprinkle with the lime juice and set aside.

In a small bowl, stir together the rum, brown sugar, cinnamon, and ginger. Pour into a large skillet and simmer on medium heat for a couple of minutes, until the sugar is melted. Add the banana slices and stir gently to coat them with the sauce. Spread out the bananas, reduce the heat, and simmer for 3 or 4 minutes, until the sauce thickens and the bananas begin to soften and fall apart. Remove from the pan and serve warm.

serving & menu ideas ∾

Served plain, these bananas hold their own as a simple dessert, or they can be dressed up with toasted coconut and a garnish of fresh mint leaves. They are also delicious as a topping on cake or vanilla ice cream. This is a fabulous dessert to follow a supper inspired by the cuisine of the Caribbean, India, or Southeast Asia, such as Spicy Potatoes & Spinach (page 45) or Roasted Vegetable Curry (page 53).

riesling roasted pears ∾

These subtly spiced pears have an attractive crinkly look and are a lovely finish for an autumn meal. They keep nicely in the refrigerator for 4 or 5 days.

SERVES 8

TIME: 50 MINUTES

8 ripe pears
zest and juice of 1 lemon
zest and juice of 1 orange
1 cup Riesling or other sweet white wine
6 peppercorns
1 cinnamon stick
$\frac{1}{2}$ cup sugar
6 whole cloves (optional)

Preheat the oven to 375°. Place the pears in a baking dish that will comfortably hold them in an upright position.

Place the rest of the ingredients in a saucepan on medium heat. Bring the mixture to a boil. To reduce the liquid a bit, cook on high heat for 5 minutes, stirring occasionally so it doesn't boil over. Pour the spiced wine over the pears and bake until the pears can be pierced easily with a sharp knife, 30 to 40 minutes. Baste once or twice, using tongs to lift a pear if necessary to get to the basting liquid.

Serve at room temperature with the wine sauce drizzled over the pears.

cherry shortbread crumble ↶

The easiest crumble we know of—it uses frozen cherries and store-bought shortbread cookies that you can find on the natural foods shelf. (See photo on page 258.)

SERVES 4

TIME: 30 MINUTES

16 ounces frozen pitted, sweet cherries without sugar or 3 cups
    pitted fresh
1 tablespoon sugar
¼ teaspoon cinnamon
1 cup crumbled shortbread cookies or pecan sandies
    (about 8 cookies)

Preheat the oven to 425°.

Put the cherries into an unoiled 8-inch square baking pan or a 9-inch glass pie plate. Sprinkle with the sugar and cinnamon and add 2 tablespoons of water to the dish. Bake for 15 minutes, and then remove from the oven. Top with the crumbled cookies and bake until the cherries are bubbling and the crumbs are browned, about 10 minutes more.

Serve warm, at room temperature, or cold.

orange-almond polenta cake ✎

Making cake batter in the blender? What could be easier? This cake is elegant enough for a dinner party and easy enough for a weekday.

SERVES 8

HANDS-ON TIME:
15 MINUTES

BAKING TIME:
45 MINUTES

⅓ cup cornmeal

⅔ cup unbleached white flour

2 teaspoons baking powder

½ teaspoon salt

1½ cups almonds

¾ cup sugar

1 orange

½ cup vegetable oil

2 eggs

confectioners' sugar for dusting

Preheat the oven to 350°. Lightly oil and flour a 9-inch round cake pan.

Sift the cornmeal, flour, baking powder, and salt into a bowl. In a blender or food processor, whirl the almonds and sugar until the almonds are finely ground. Add to the flour mixture.

Grate the orange peel (see page 290) and juice the orange (about ⅓ cup). Add the orange juice, orange zest, oil, eggs, and ⅓ cup of water to the blender or food processor and whirl for about 15 seconds. Add the dry ingredients and blend until well mixed, using a spatula to scrape down the sides if necessary. Pour the batter into the prepared pan and bake for about 45 minutes, until a toothpick inserted in the center of the cake comes out clean.

Cool on a rack for 10 minutes; then carefully remove the cake from the pan. When thoroughly cool, dust with confectioners' sugar.

INGREDIENT NOTE If you don't have a fresh orange, this cake will be just fine with ⅓ cup prepared orange juice.

serving & menu ideas ✎

Serve with berries or sliced fruit such as peaches or nectarines.

peach brown betty

Old-fashioned and still delicious.

SERVES 8

HANDS-ON TIME:
20 MINUTES

BAKING TIME:
20 MINUTES

16 ounces frozen sliced peaches (4 cups)

¼ cup butter (½ stick)

1 egg

¼ cup milk or half-and-half

2 teaspoons vanilla

1 teaspoon ground cinnamon

1 cup packed brown sugar

½ loaf of crusty bread such as Italian, French, or challah
(about 8 ounces)

Preheat the oven to 400°. Butter a 2-quart baking dish.

In a covered saucepan on low heat or in a microwave oven, heat the frozen peaches just until bubbling and beginning to give off juice. When the peaches are hot, add the butter and stir to melt. Meanwhile, in a large bowl, beat the egg well. Whisk in the milk, vanilla, cinnamon, and ½ cup of the brown sugar. Cut the bread into ½-inch cubes (7 to 8 cups) and add to the bowl. Add the hot peaches and melted butter to the bowl and toss well.

Spread the Peach Brown Betty into the baking dish and sprinkle with the rest of the brown sugar. Bake uncovered for about 20 minutes, until bubbling and golden brown. Serve warm or at room temperature.

variation

Add a cup of fresh or frozen blueberries, raspberries, or blackberries to the bowl after you add the peaches and toss gently to distribute well.

chocolate ricotta pudding ∾

*A protein-rich, almost instant, smooth, deep chocolate dessert.
Nice garnished with red raspberries or strawberries.*

SERVES 4 TO 6

TIME: 10 MINUTES

6 ounces semi-sweet chocolate (1 cup of chips)

15 or 16 ounces ricotta cheese

1 teaspoon vanilla

1 cup heavy cream

2 tablespoons confectioners' sugar

Melt the chocolate in a small pan, on very low heat, taking care not to scorch it. Or melt it in a microwave oven. In a blender or a food processor, whirl the ricotta, vanilla, and melted chocolate until smooth and evenly colored. Pour into dessert cups (leave space for whipped cream). Refrigerate until ready to serve.

When you're ready to serve, in a small bowl with an electric mixer or a whisk, whip the cream and the confectioners' sugar until stiff. Mound the whipped cream on top of the pudding and serve cold.

mango coconut sorbet ∿

Creamy, fruity, refreshing, and vegan. The combination of mango and coconut makes this a perfect dessert to follow a Caribbean or Indian meal.

SERVES 4 TO 6

HANDS-ON TIME:
15 MINUTES

FREEZING TIME:
AT LEAST 4 HOURS

HANDS-ON TIME JUST
BEFORE SERVING:
10 MINUTES

2 ripe mangoes

1 cup coconut milk

¼ cup sugar

Peel and pit the mangoes and cut them into chunks. Place the mangoes in the bowl of a food processor, add the coconut milk and sugar, and whirl until smooth. Ladle or pour the purée into two ice cube trays. Freeze for at least 4 hours.

When ready to serve, release the frozen cubes and allow them to soften at room temperature for about 5 minutes. (They should be soft enough to facilitate puréeing, but not melted.) Purée in a food processor until smooth, in batches if necessary.

planning tip ∿

The sorbet purée can be made ahead, frozen in cubes, and kept in the freezer for up to 2 weeks. Keep the frozen cubes in a freezer bag until ready to serve.

mocha sorbet ∾

The richness of this dark, not-too-sweet sorbet belies the simplicity of its ingredients and ease of preparation. Serve it as a lovely dessert, or use it as a pick-me-up on a hot afternoon. The refreshing iciness and the chocolate-coffee flavor are especially good after Mexican food.

SERVES 4

HANDS-ON TIME:
10 MINUTES

FREEZING TIME:
AT LEAST 4 HOURS

HANDS-ON TIME JUST
BEFORE SERVING:
10 MINUTES

$^2/_3$ cup semi-sweet chocolate chips

$^1/_4$ cup sugar

2 cups espresso (brewed or instant)

whipped cream (optional)

In a small, heavy saucepan on low heat, melt the chocolate chips and sugar in the espresso, stirring frequently. Ladle or pour the mocha mixture into two ice cube trays and freeze for at least 4 hours.

When ready to serve, release the cubes and allow them to soften at room temperature for about 5 minutes. (They should be soft enough to facilitate puréeing, but not melted.) In a food processor, whirl the cubes until smooth, in batches if necessary. Serve immediately, topped with whipped cream if you like.

planning tip ∾

The mocha mixture can be made ahead, frozen in cubes, and kept in the freezer for up to 2 weeks. Keep the frozen cubes in a freezer bag until ready to serve.

caramel custard ∾

A can of dulce de leche *is the key to this smooth, rich, caramel-flavored custard that you can make with only 10 minutes of prep time. It would take hours to make the milk caramel you can purchase ready-made in many supermarkets. The cans are usually shelved with other Latin American foods and called Dulce de Leche, Manjar, Fanguito, Arequíte, or Cajeta.*

SERVES 6 TO 10

HANDS-ON TIME:
10 MINUTES

BAKING TIME:
35 MINUTES

1 13.4-ounce can of *dulce de leche*

6 large eggs

2 cups milk

pinch of salt

sprinkling of nutmeg or cinnamon (optional)

Preheat the oven to 350°. Arrange ten 4-ounce or seven 6-ounce custard cups in a baking pan(s) at least 2 inches deep. Bring a teakettle of water to boil.

In a blender or with an electric mixer, beat the *dulce de leche,* eggs, milk, and salt until smooth and evenly colored (about 10 seconds in a blender, or 1 or 2 minutes with a mixer). Pour into the custard cups. Sprinkle with nutmeg or cinnamon.

When the water boils, pour it into the baking pan to come three-quarters of the way up the sides of the custard cups. Carefully place the baking pan in the oven and bake the custards for about 35 minutes, until a knife inserted in the center of a custard comes out clean. Remove the custards from the water bath so they won't continue to cook. Serve warm, at room temperature, or chilled.

serving & menu ideas ∾

This custard is a perfect end to a Mexican, Latin American, or Caribbean-style meal, such as Nachos Grandes (page 63), Black Beans with Pickled Red Onions (page 58), or West Indian Red Beans & Coconut Rice (page 69).

banana cupcakes ᘓ

Sweet-smelling, dense, and moist, these cupcakes don't really need a frosting—it's just icing on the cake! And yes, they really do taste good made with olive oil. These cupcakes are good keepers; they stay moist for up to a week.

**YIELDS ABOUT
20 CUPCAKES**

HANDS-ON TIME:
CAKE: 15 MINUTES
FROSTING: 10 MINUTES

BAKING TIME:
20 TO 25 MINUTES

COOLING TIME:
AT LEAST 15 MINUTES

WET INGREDIENTS

1½ cups mashed ripe bananas (3 or 4 bananas)

½ cup olive oil or vegetable oil

1⅓ cups packed brown sugar

3 eggs

1 teaspoon vanilla

¼ cup plain yogurt

DRY INGREDIENTS

1½ cups unbleached white flour

1 teaspoon baking soda

½ teaspoon salt

COFFEE OR CHOCOLATE CREAM CHEESE FROSTING

8 ounces cream cheese, at room temperature

3 tablespoons butter, at room temperature

1 cup sifted confectioners' sugar

2 tablespoons brewed coffee or 1 tablespoon cocoa powder

Preheat the oven to 350°. Prepare two standard cupcake pans with liners, cooking spray, or butter.

With an electric mixer on medium speed, mix the wet ingredients until smooth and creamy, a minute or two. In a separate bowl, sift together the dry ingredients. Add the dry ingredients to the wet ingredients and mix at low speed until smooth. Spoon the batter into the cupcake pans, filling each cup about three-quarters full. Bake until a toothpick inserted in the center of a cupcake comes out clean, 20 to 25 minutes.

Meanwhile, mix all of the frosting ingredients with an electric mixer on low speed until creamy and smooth. Cool the cupcakes for at least 15 minutes and then frost.

planning tip ∿

If you have bananas that are overripe and you don't have time to bake, pop them unpeeled into the freezer. Later, thaw the bananas for use in a recipe.

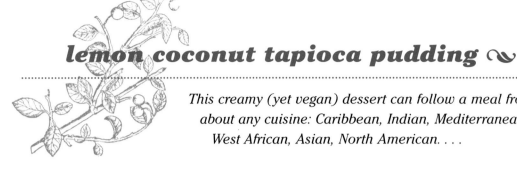

lemon coconut tapioca pudding ∾

This creamy (yet vegan) dessert can follow a meal from just
about any cuisine: Caribbean, Indian, Mediterranean,
West African, Asian, North American. . . .

SERVES 4

TIME: 25 MINUTES

¼ cup quick-cooking tapioca

¼ teaspoon salt

5 tablespoons sugar

1 14-ounce can of coconut milk

1 teaspoon grated lemon peel

Place the tapioca, salt, and sugar in a medium saucepan, stir in ½ cup of cool water, and set aside for 5 minutes. Then stir in the coconut milk and bring to a simmer on high heat. Reduce the heat to low and cook, stirring often to prevent sticking, until thick and creamy, about 10 minutes.

Stir in the lemon peel. Pour into dessert dishes and serve warm, at room temperature, or chilled.

serving & menu ideas ∾

Just before serving, top with sliced fresh fruit—our favorite is mango. Ripe, fresh mango can't be beat, but good canned mango is available, too. Strawberries, peaches, cherries, or pineapple are also delicious as a topping.

new england squash pie ∽

This pie is lighter in flavor and texture than its pumpkin cousins.
If you've got a pie shell waiting, it's a snap to get this treat
into the oven.

SERVES 8

HANDS-ON TIME:
10 MINUTES

BAKING TIME:
30 TO 40 MINUTES

1 11-ounce package of frozen cooked winter squash

1¼ cups milk

3 eggs

¾ cup sugar

1 teaspoon vanilla

¼ teaspoon salt

1 teaspoon ground cinnamon

¼ teaspoon nutmeg

pinch of ground cloves

1 unbaked 9- or 10-inch pie shell (thawed, if frozen)

Preheat the oven to 350°.

Warm the squash in a microwave oven or in a pot on top of the stove. Place it in a blender or mixing bowl with the milk, eggs, sugar, vanilla, salt, and spices and whirl, or whisk by hand, until smooth.

Place the pie shell on a baking tray and pour the filling into it. (Purchased pie crusts vary in depth, so if you have too much filling for your crust, put the extra in a custard cup or ramekin and follow the directions in the note below.)

Bake for 30 to 40 minutes, until the the filling is set but there is still a little jiggle in the center. Cool at room temperature for at least 30 minutes before serving.

INGREDIENT NOTES Good frozen pie shells, including wheat-free ones, are available in natural foods stores and large supermarkets.

For custard instead of pie, bake the filling in unbuttered custard cups set in a hot water bath. Depending on the size of your cups, this recipe will make 4 to 8 custards. Bake for 15 to 25 minutes, until just set. Cool at room temperature for at least 15 minutes before serving.

butterscotch icebox cookies ∾

This cookie dough can be kept in the freezer for up to at least two months, so whenever you want warm, freshly baked cookies (with none of the additives found in commercially prepared frozen cookie dough), just slice it and pop it in the oven.

YIELDS ABOUT 6 DOZEN COOKIES

HANDS-ON TIME:
15 MINUTES

FREEZING TIME:
AT LEAST 1 HOUR

BAKING TIME:
8 TO 12 MINUTES
PER BATCH

1 cup butter, at room temperature

2 cups packed brown sugar

2 eggs

1 teaspoon vanilla

½ teaspoon salt

3 cups unbleached white flour

In a mixing bowl, cream the butter and brown sugar with an electric mixer until fluffy. Beat in the eggs, vanilla, and salt. Mix in the flour until well blended.

Divide the dough into 3 parts. Shape each third into a log about 1½ inches in diameter and 8 inches long. Wrap the logs with waxed paper or plastic wrap and place in the freezer until firm, at least 1 hour. (If the dough will be stored for more than a day, place the wrapped logs in a sealed freezer bag, label, and date.)

When you're ready to bake, preheat the oven to 375°. With a sharp knife, slice the logs into rounds about ¼ inch thick. Place 1 inch apart on an unoiled baking sheet. Bake for 8 to 12 minutes, until the cookies retain a slight indentation when lightly touched in the center and are golden brown on the bottom. Remove the cookies from the baking sheet while they're still warm.

INGREDIENT NOTES For crisper cookies, add ¾ teaspoon of baking soda with the flour.

For puffier cookies, add 1 tablespoon of baking powder with the flour.

serving & menu ideas ∾

For delicious sandwich cookies, spread peanut butter or Nutella between the bottoms of two cooled cookies.

two sweet sauces ❧

These two sauces are useful whenever you need to make a dessert in a hurry. Made in minutes, they can turn plain ice cream or store-bought poundcake into something special.

peanut butter chocolate sauce

You can make this sauce ahead of time and store it in the refrigerator. When ready to serve, reheat, stirring frequently, until melted.

YIELDS 1½ CUPS

TIME: 10 MINUTES

1 cup semi-sweet chocolate chips
2 tablespoons sugar
½ cup water or milk
1 teaspoon vanilla
¼ cup creamy or crunchy peanut butter

In a double boiler or a heatproof bowl over a pan of simmering water, melt the chocolate chips and sugar in the water or milk, stirring with a whisk until smooth and shiny. Whisk in the vanilla and peanut butter.

blueberry lemon sauce

This twilight-blue sweet-tart sauce will keep in the refrigerator for up to a week. Made in a food processor, it's thicker than when made in the blender.

YIELDS 2 CUPS

TIME: 10 MINUTES

1 pound frozen or fresh blueberries
   (about 3 cups)
⅓ cup sugar
pinch of salt
2 teaspoons lemon juice

In a saucepan on medium heat, bring the blueberries, sugar, salt, and a tablespoon of water to a simmer, stirring often, until the mixture is juicy. Cook for a few minutes, until the blueberries are soft.

In a blender or food processor, whirl the blueberries with the lemon juice until smooth. Add additional sugar to taste. Add more water if you want a thinner sauce.

5-minute milkshakes ∾

Whip up one of these pretty pastel shakes for a casual dessert or any time you finish supper wishing you had made dessert. We suggest Chai Shake after a curry, Vanilla Rum Milkshake after West Indian Red Beans & Coconut Rice (page 69), Pineapple Ginger Shake after Asian Braised Fish with Greens (page 160)—you get the picture.

SERVES 2

TIME: 5 MINUTES

In a blender, purée the ingredients until smooth, about 30 seconds. Pour into small glasses and serve immediately.

orange vanilla shake

1 cup orange juice

1 cup vanilla ice cream

1 teaspoon grated orange peel (optional)

chocolate malt

1 cup vanilla ice cream

2 tablespoons chocolate syrup

¼ cup Ovaltine or other malt powder

¾ cup milk

vanilla rum milkshake

1 cup vanilla ice cream

2 tablespoons rum

1 cup milk

2 tablespoons brown sugar

grated nutmeg for sprinkling on top

banana milkshake

1 cup vanilla ice cream

1 cup milk

1 ripe banana

ground cinnamon or grated nutmeg for sprinkling on top

chai shake

1 cup vanilla ice cream

1 cup chilled chai (look for aseptic boxes on supermarket shelves near the soy milk)

pineapple ginger shake

½ cup pineapple juice

1 cup vanilla ice cream

½ teaspoon peeled and grated ginger root

1 tablespoon lime juice

the well-stocked pantry

When your pantry is stocked with interesting foods and your freezer is full, you can eat well without a trip to the market. The authors of *Simple Suppers* are all Moosewood cooks, and there are plenty of days when we don't want supper at home to be a major culinary production. A little time in the kitchen, yes. Creative? Maybe. Masterful? We hope. Time-consuming? No. Some days we have a hankering for something in particular and so we stop at the store, but most days when it's time for dinner we check what's in the cupboard and refrigerator and pull out our favorite simple supper ingredients.

Each of us has different favorite staples, items that may not have been in our pantries a few years ago but that we regularly use for convenience and good taste today. Our current collective top-ten list of favorites for convenience in our home kitchens includes little cans of smoky-hot chipotle peppers packed in flavorful adobo sauce, frozen edamame, bags of refrigerated slaw mix, quart boxes of organic vegetable broth, Chinese chili paste, Thai curry paste, frozen collards, cans of diced tomatoes, Keiffer lime leaves in freezer bags, and seasoned tofu.

Here is a more extensive, but not exhaustive, list of things you might find in the home kitchen of a Moosewood cook for the recipes in this book and beyond.

In the Cupboard

Quart boxes of organic vegetable, mushroom, and mock chicken broth (see page 295); canned whole and diced tomatoes; salsa (we recommend Herdez and Pace brands); chipotles in adobo sauce; peanut butter; artichoke hearts; coconut milk; roasted red peppers; jams or fruit spreads; oils (olive oil, extra-virgin olive oil, vegetable or canola oil, dark sesame oil); vinegars (cider, wine, white, balsamic, rice);

beans and peas (black beans, black-eyed peas, butter beans, cannellini, chickpeas, small red beans, field peas—we recommend Goya, Cora Natural, The Allens, Westbrae, and Eden brands of canned beans); dry lentils (red, green, French); dry split peas (yellow, green); raisins and currants; hijiki seaweed, sun-dried tomatoes; dried mushrooms (porcini, shiitake, cremini).

Spices and Dried Herbs

Red pepper flakes, cayenne, allspice, cinnamon, nutmeg, cardamom, ginger, curry powder, garam masala, turmeric, saffron, paprika, Old Bay seasoning, bay leaves, sage, rosemary, thyme, tarragon, oregano, basil, dill, mint (we use spearmint and peppermint herbal teas), cumin, coriander, fennel, and black mustard seeds.

Grains

Rice (brown, jasmine, basmati, arborio, white), polenta cornmeal, grits, couscous, kasha, bulghur, quinoa.

Pasta

Italian pasta (fettuccine, spaghetti, linguine, orzo, farfalle, penne, etc.—see page 291), rice noodles, soba noodles, udon noodles.

In the Refrigerator

Mayonnaise, mustard, horseradish, barbecue sauce, hoisin sauce, Tabasco or other hot sauce, soy sauce, Chinese chili paste, Thai curry paste, olives, pickles and/or relish, capers, tofu, seitan, miso, fresh ginger root and garlic, nuts and seeds (walnuts, pecans, almonds, cashews, pine nuts, peanuts, sesame seeds), various cheeses, butter, eggs, yogurt, slaw mix.

In the Freezer

Tortillas, filo dough, Keiffer lime leaves, tortellini, corn, collards, spinach, edamame, black-eyed peas, green peas, shrimp.

guide to ingredients, tools & techniques

This guide is not exhaustive. Rather, it includes practical information about some of the ingredients, tools, and techniques specific to recipes in this book.

AVOCADOS: We use Hass avocados, a variety with dark green pebbly skin and a smooth yellowish-green interior. A hard avocado will usually ripen and soften and be ready to eat in 3 to 4 days at room temperature. To cube an avocado, use a paring knife to slice down to the pit around the avocado lengthwise. Gently twist the halves apart and remove the pit. Cut the flesh in a crisscross pattern right in the skins, and scoop out the cubes with a spoon.

BLACK MUSTARD SEEDS: To draw out the nutty flavor of this Indian spice, briefly heat the seeds in a dry skillet on medium heat and then grind them. Or sauté them in a small amount of oil until they begin to pop. Look for them in Indian or Asian markets or in well-stocked supermarkets.

BOK CHOY (CHINESE CABBAGE, PAK CHOI, BAK CHOI): Like celery, bok choy stalks grow from a single base and branch into white crisp stalks with broad deep green leaves. Eat both the leaves and the stalks.

CAPERS: The tiny, green buds of a flowering Mediterranean plant, capers are packed either in a vinegar-based brine or in sea salt. At Moosewood, we use the brine-packed variety. Rinse salted capers before using.

CHEESE:

ASADERO is a good melting cheese and an alternative to Muenster and Monterey Jack. Asadero is perfect for quesadillas and other Mexican dishes.

BLUE CHEESES are marbled with blue or green veins depending on the molds introduced during cheese making. They come in a wide variety of strengths and textures. The main types include Italian Gorgonzola, Danish blue cheese, English Stilton, French Roquefort, and domestic blue cheese made in Canada and the United States. Most are made with cow's milk, except Roquefort, which is always made with sheep's milk.

BRIE is a ripened cheese with an edible white mold rind. It has a smooth, buttery texture and flavor.

CHEDDAR, both mild and sharp, is widely available and versatile.

CHÈVRE is a smooth and slightly tangy fresh goat cheese.

HAVARTI, named after a farm in Denmark, is a semi-soft, creamy cheese with small irregular holes. Dilled Havarti is flecked with dill.

FETA is a salty, white cheese made from sheep's, goats', or cows' milk. It varies from mild and creamy to quite sharp.

FONTINA, mild but distinctly flavored, is made in Denmark and the United States.

FRESH MOZZARELLA is mild, creamy cheese that comes in balls packed in water. Look for it in the dairy case or in supermarket delis or salad bars.

GRUYÈRE is a delicious, dense, nutty cheese.

NEUFCHÂTEL has one-third less fat than cream cheese, without sacrificing texture or flavor. Neufchâtel is what we most often use when a recipe calls for cream cheese.

PARMESAN is a firm, aged cheese, best when freshly shaved, shredded, or grated.

PECORINO ROMANO, made from sheep's milk, is usually stronger and sharper than Parmesan. Like Parmesan, grate it fresh.

RICOTTA, traditionally used in Italian cooking for both sweet and savory dishes, is soft, fresh, and mild-tasting, with a creamy texture. Ricotta cheese is available as a whole milk, reduced fat, or nonfat product.

RICOTTA SALATA is salted, pressed ricotta, a firm cheese with a dry texture.

SMOKED CHEESES are infused with a smoky flavor either by exposure to a hickory wood fire, by the addition of smoked salt, or by adding a chemical called *liquid smoke* during cheesemaking. The most readily available smoked cheeses are

Cheddar, Gouda, Swiss, and Mozzarella. Look for naturally smoked cheeses in natural foods stores and gourmet cheese shops.

SOY CHEESE is a vegan alternative to cheese made with dairy milk. Developed over the past 15 years, new soy cheese products that approximate a particular type of cheese, such as Cheddar or Parmesan, appear in our market often.

CHILES (HOT PEPPERS, CHILI PEPPERS): There are many, many types of chiles, and their heat varies wildly even among chiles of the same type, so taste to determine how much to use. For less heat, remove the seeds and membrane, which are the hottest parts. Refrigerated in a plastic bag, fresh chiles will keep for about 5 days. Frozen whole chiles can be kept for up to a year; sliced or chopped, for 6 months.

CHINESE CHILI PASTE: Supermarkets usually carry a wide variety of chili pastes, most of which include crushed, fermented chiles, salt, soy oil, and garlic. We've found that the simpler the ingredient list, the better. Look for bottled brands without preservatives. Tightly capped and refrigerated, Chinese chili paste keeps indefinitely. If you don't have Chinese chili paste, substitute pressed garlic and some minced fresh chile pepper.

CHIPOTLES IN ADOBO SAUCE, usually packed in small cans, are whole smoked jalapeños in a thick, flavorful tomato sauce called *adobo* that usually contains tomatoes, vinegar, onions, ground chiles, sugar, spices, and herbs. The peppers are hotter than the sauce; we use only the sauce when we want a mellow yet flavorful smokiness. We like La Torre brand canned chipotles in adobo sauce.

CHUTNEY is a sweet-and-sour Indian condiment made with fruit, vegetables, and spices. Chutney is easily made (see recipes on pages 229 and 231), but a wide variety of prepared chutneys is available in the gourmet, Indian, or Asian aisle of most supermarkets.

COCONUT MILK, smooth, thick, and richly flavored, is made from water and grated coconut that has been puréed and strained. It comes canned in regular and reduced-fat versions and is available free of preservatives and additives. Once the can is opened, the coconut milk will keep for about 3 days in the refrigerator. Frozen, it will last indefinitely. Pour leftover coconut milk into ice-cube trays and freeze it. Later, store the frozen cubes in a freezer bag; cubes dropped into soups and sauces melt easily and quickly.

COOKING SPRAYS (oil in a spray can) are very convenient. They make oiling baking dishes a snap. Look for pure olive oil or canola oil sprays, or find an oil spray jar in cooking stores and use your own oil.

CURRY PASTE is a Southeast Asian condiment that combines curry spices and vegetable oils to create a highly concentrated seasoning. Like curry powders, curry pastes have a range of flavors and spiciness. Curry pastes are available in jars at Indian groceries and in the Indian or Southeast Asian section of many supermarkets.

EDAMAME are shelled or unshelled fresh or frozen soybeans. Look for edamame in the produce department or among the frozen vegetables.

FENNEL (fennel bulb, anise) is a curious-looking vegetable with a sweet anise flavor and crunchy texture. Fresh fennel has a large, white, edible, bulbous bottom with green celery-like stalks topped by feathery fronds. The bulb is usually sliced, and the fronds make nice garnishes. The tough stalks should be discarded.

GINGER ROOT is a knobby, light brown rhizome with a clear, fresh scent and hot, spicy taste. Look for it in the produce section of food markets. If the skin is very thin and tender, there is no need to peel it before grating it (a microplane grater is the best; see page 290). If the skin is blemished or tough, peel it first with a paring knife or vegetable peeler or by scraping it with the edge of a spoon.

GREENS

Greens is a term that refers to both raw salad greens and to cooked leafy greens. Popular salad greens include Boston lettuce, spinach, Belgian endive, mesclun (field mix, spring mix), loose-leaf lettuces, radicchio, and arugula. Cooked greens include chard, collards, escarole, kale, mustard greens, broccoli raab, bok choy, and watercress. We always rinse bagged and bulk salad greens, even when labeled prewashed.

> **ARUGULA** becomes more peppery and sharp-tasting as it matures. Arugula is used both as a cooked green and raw in salads.

> **CHARD:** We use both red-veined ruby chard and green Swiss chard. Look for fresh perky leaves with bright tender stems and veins.

> **COLLARDS** (collard greens) are mild-tasting, bluish-green, paddle-shaped leaves.

To strip collards, hold a leaf by the stem, grasp the base of the leaf with your other hand, and pull your hands away from each other, stripping off the leaf. Frozen collards are widely available and are convenient and have pretty good flavor. They cook more quickly than most fresh collards. One pound of raw collards yields about 4 cups cooked.

ENDIVE (frisée, curly endive) is a delicate, bitter salad green with frilly leaves and a crisp texture. It will keep fresh in the refrigerator for about 3 days. Rinse well before using.

ESCAROLE has mildly bitter, dark green, wavy leaves with white sweet-tasting midribs. Avoid wilted, yellow, or brown-edged bunches. Escarole will keep in a perforated plastic bag for several days in the refrigerator.

KALE, an exceptionally nutritious food, is available in several varieties. The most common varieties have bluish-green, frilly-edged leaves or smooth purplish-red leaves. Kale will keep in the refrigerator for at least a week. To strip kale leaves, hold each leaf by the stem, grasp the base of the leaf with your other hand, and pull your hands away from each other, stripping off the leaf. One pound of raw kale yields about 4 cups cooked.

MESCLUN (field mix, spring mix), a combination of various sweet, sharp, and peppery baby salad greens, such as lettuce, baby spinach, mizuna, and mustard greens, is available in bags or in bulk in most supermarket produce departments.

MUSTARD GREENS are a spicy, mustardy green, terrific for flavoring and good as a companion to milder greens such as collards or spinach. Young red mustard greens are often included in mixes of mesclun or baby greens. Wrapped in a damp towel in plastic in the refrigerator, mustard greens will keep for about 3 days.

SPINACH: We like baby spinach for its timesaving convenience: no stemming and chopping. If you use regular spinach in a recipe calling for baby spinach, remove the large stems and coarsely chop the leaves, and then measure it. Buy frozen spinach that is packaged in bags rather than in blocks, because in bags the spinach is frozen in separate clumps, so portions can be easily removed and the bag resealed.

HERBS, FRESH AND DRIED: The scent, bright color, and fresh flavor of a fresh herb can make the simplest dish delectable, but dried herbs work better in some dishes. As a rule of thumb, use about half the amount of dried as fresh herbs. To test for strength of flavor, rub a pinch of dried herb between your fingers and breathe in the scent. Adjust the amount you use according to the intensity of the aroma.

HOISIN SAUCE, a sweet Chinese condiment, is a deep chocolate-colored purée with a smooth, thick texture. It usually contains soybeans, sugar, vinegar, and spices.

HORSERADISH: A pungent condiment. Most supermarkets carry jars of grated horse-radish mixed with vinegar and salt.

IMMERSION BLENDER: A lightweight electric blender with a shaft that can be immersed in hot soups or sauces right in the pot. They save time and cleanup (and are safer than pouring hot soup into a blender jar). Also, you can use them to blend whole tomatoes right in the can.

KEIFFER LIME LEAVES (kafir lime leaves, magroot, makrug, wild limes), used in Thai and Indonesian cuisine, are the glossy, dark green leaves of a tree grown in Southeast Asia and Hawaii. They have a unique lemon-lime perfume and wonderful flavor. Whole leaves, like bay leaves, are used to flavor hot foods and then discarded before eating. When finely shredded, they can be eaten cooked and raw. Keiffer lime leaves freeze well—just place dry whole leaves in a freezer bag, and they'll retain flavor for months. Look for them in the produce section of large supermarkets.

KITCHEN SCISSORS: Buy sharp kitchen scissors to snip fresh herbs into neat, finely chopped garnishes; to trim the sharp points from fresh artichoke leaves; to cut cooked noodles and parchment paper; to create vegetable, flower, and fruit decorations. Carefully dry the blades after washing to keep the scissors from rusting.

LEMONGRASS STALKS are amazingly aromatic reeds, treasured more for their fragrance than their flavor. They can grow up to 2 feet high and range in color from pale yellowish green to green-gray. To use lemongrass, cut off the tough root end, peel away the thick outer layers, and slice or mince the tender core. The tough exterior layers can be used in stock. Lemongrass is sold in Asian markets and many supermarkets. It is easy to grow, and although tropical, it will grow in moderate climates, and we have successfully harvested it even with our short upstate New York summers.

MANGOES: There is nothing quite like a luscious ripe mango. Mangoes have a large, flat central pit that occupies about a third of the fruit and the pulp is very slippery, so be careful when slicing or peeling them. To cube a mango, use a sharp knife and slice from top to bottom along one of the broad, flat sides, cutting as close to the pit as possible. Then slice off the other side, leaving about a 1-inch strip of pulp and peel attached to the pit. Without cutting into the peel, score the pulp of each sliced half in a crosshatch pattern. Then bend each mango half inside out and slice off the cubes. Carefully peel and then cut away the pulp clinging to the pit.

MICROPLANE GRATER: Possibly the greatest cooking tool introduced in the last decade. A long, flat stainless-steel grater with small, sharp grating edges. It makes fast work of grating whole nutmeg, fresh ginger and hard cheeses, and it's perfect for grating lemon and orange peel; with a light touch, the zest is very finely shredded (not gummy), and it's easy to avoid grating too deep and getting into the bitter pith. Microplane graters are easy to use and easy to clean. Originally they were woodworking tools sold in hardware stores, and then someone discovered how great they are in the kitchen. Look for them in kitchen supply stores and cooking catalogs.

MIRIN: A Japanese sweet cooking wine made from rice, with a lovely, sweet flavor. If you're caught without mirin, substitute brown sugar (two-thirds of the amount of mirin called for) or a mixture of two-thirds dry sherry and one-third brown sugar. Find mirin where Japanese foods are sold.

MISO: A salty, fermented soybean-grain paste. Types vary greatly in intensity and flavor depending on the grains added to the soybeans and the length of the aging process. We most often use rice miso, which is amber-colored and has a delicate and slightly sweet flavor. Add miso at the end of cooking. Avoid boiling it, because high heat destroys its beneficial digestive and antibacterial enzymes. Miso is available in natural foods stores, most supermarkets, and Asian groceries where Japanese foods are sold.

NUTS

We recommend whole nuts and pieces because they're less expensive than prepackaged chopped or sliced ones, and their flavor is superior when you chop them as they're needed. Nuts should be kept in the refrigerator for short-term storage, or frozen in freezer bags and containers for up to a year.

To toast nuts:

IN A MICROWAVE OVEN: Nuts and seeds don't brown in a microwave, but they do get that crispness and the deep, rich flavor of oven-toasted nuts. Spread the nuts on a plate; the time varies for different nuts and depending on the strength of the microwave oven.

IN A SKILLET: In a heavy skillet on medium heat, spread the nuts in one layer and toast, stirring as they brown. They're done when they become aromatic and lightly browned.

IN THE OVEN: Preheat the oven to 350°. Spread the nuts or seeds evenly in one layer on a dry baking sheet. Bake them for about 5 minutes, stirring once for even toasting.

OLD BAY is our favorite brand of Chesapeake Bay seasoning, a distinctive spice and herb mix, salty with a hint of heat, commonly used in seafood dishes. Usually, you'll find it near the seafood counter or in the spice section.

PAPPADAMS are round, flat, extremely thin disks about 8 inches in diameter, made of spiced chickpea or lentil flour, and commonly used in Indian cooking. Cook each pappadam by briefly frying in a heavy skillet in hot oil. As soon as it is placed in the hot oil, it will brown, blister, and become crisp. Remove right away and place on paper towels to drain. Packages of pappadams can be bought in Asian groceries or the international section of supermarkets.

PASTA: For cooking directions, see page 17. Italian pasta is made in a multitude of shapes: long strands (spaghetti, fusilli, linguine, fettuccine), short and chunky (spiralini, farfalle, elbows, short penne), flat (fettuccine, farfalle, lasagna noodles, tagliatelle), hollowed (penne, ziti, elbows, shells, orecchiette) and very short or small (pastina, orzo, tubettini, gnocchetti sardi). Most of the Italian names for the shapes are descriptive, sometimes amusing: orecchiette, little ears; spaghetti, strings; tubetti and tubettini, small tubes and tiny tubes; linguine, tongues; farfalle, butterflies; manicotti, small muffs. It's a good thing that pasta comes in clear bags, so we can see what we're getting.

PESTO is a sumptuous paste usually made with olive oil, basil, nuts, garlic, and aged cheese. Homemade pesto freezes very well. In specialty food stores and often in the produce section of supermarkets, you can find pesto packed in jars—a great pantry staple for last-minute meals.

PINE NUTS (pignoli) are the edible seeds of certain pine trees that grow in Central America, the Mediterranean, and southwestern United States. These highly perishable nuts have a sweet flavor and creamy texture. Store them in a closed container in the refrigerator for up to 2 months. For the best flavor, dry-roast them in a skillet or 350° oven for 3 to 5 minutes until golden brown.

ROASTED RED PEPPERS: Look for roasted red peppers in jars or cans in Italian grocery stores or near the pasta sauces in supermarkets. To roast a fresh pepper, place a whole red bell pepper directly over the flame on a gas stove or under the broiler and char it for about 10 minutes, turning occasionally with tongs. Cool the pepper in a covered bowl or a closed paper bag. Remove the stem and seeds and most of the charred skin.

RICE: See page 176.

RICE NOODLES (rice sticks) are long, translucent, off-white noodles of various widths, round and flat. They're made of rice flour. Look for them in Asian groceries and many supermarkets. To cook rice noodles, either boil them briefly in plenty of water or immerse them in hot water and let them sit for several minutes, until soft.

SALAD GREENS: See *Greens*, page 287.

SEASONED TOFU: See *Tofu*, page 294.

SEITAN: Wheat gluten that has been boiled and then sautéed in flavorings such as soy sauce and ginger. It is available in sealed packages and canned, both plain and seasoned, and once opened will keep in the refrigerator for about a week.

SESAME OIL: When we call for sesame oil in this book, we mean dark sesame oil, which is pressed from roasted sesame seeds and is used as a rich, aromatic flavoring.

SHRIMP: The count on shrimp labels refers to how many shrimp of that size are in 1 pound. The smaller the count, the larger the shrimp. Usually larger shrimp are more succulent and flavorful but more expensive, too. Shrimp recipes in this book call for raw peeled and deveined shrimp. We recommend thawing frozen shrimp briefly in cold water to reduce curling and toughening when they are cooked. Shrimp are done as soon as they turn pink, usually 3 minutes in hot liquid or 3 to 5 minutes in a pan or on a hot grill; longer cooking times make them tough and dry.

SLAW MIXES: One of our favorite simple supper convenience foods, good for both quickly prepared side salads and as an ingredient in vegetable sautés. Cellophane packages of coleslaw (shredded cabbage and carrots), Asian slaw (finely shredded napa or savoy cabbage, celery, and carrots), and broccoli slaw (shredded broccoli, carrots, and celery) can be found in most supermarket produce sections.

SOBA NOODLES are hearty Japanese noodles made with buckwheat flour. Look for them in natural foods stores, Asian groceries, and large supermarkets. Cook soba noodles in a large pot of boiling water, until tender but still firm, from 3 to 10 minutes.

SOY MILK is a thick dairy-free beverage that can be used in place of regular milk in most recipes. Whole soy milk, low-fat, and flavored varieties are available in natural foods stores and supermarkets.

SOY SAUCE: The best-tasting, purest soy sauces are made from four ingredients only: soybeans, water, wheat, and salt. Some good wheat-free and low-sodium soy sauces are available. Avoid diluted sauces that include caramel coloring, sweetening, and/or preservatives. Soy sauces vary in strength and saltiness, so taste yours before adding it to a dish. Soy sauce is widely available in Asian groceries and supermarkets.

SPICE GRINDER: Ground spices are convenient, but freshly ground seeds such as fennel, cumin, coriander, and cardamom are more flavorful. An electric coffee grinder, used just for spices, makes it easy to grind as needed.

SUN-DRIED TOMATOES, with their intense tart-sweet, salty flavor and chewy texture, add an instant depth of flavor to soups, sauces, pasta, and sandwiches. They are often quite salty, so use additional salt judiciously. Look for plain dried tomatoes without sulfites. Soak dried tomatoes in boiling water for 10 to 15 minutes, until softened, before chopping and adding to a dish.

TABASCO is one of the most widely known and used brands of hot pepper sauce and a staple in the Moosewood kitchen. It's made with vinegar, red chiles, and salt. Other hot pepper sauces abound; we like to look for locally produced favorites.

TOFU, also known as bean curd, is made from soy milk to which a coagulant is added. It has little taste of its own, but it absorbs flavors readily. It comes in blocks of varying weights and firmness. Fresh tofu is packed in water and found in the refrigerator case in natural foods stores, supermarkets, and Asian grocery stores. Tofu can also be purchased in vacuum-packed containers with an indefinite shelf life at room temperature. Once the package is opened, tofu is perishable and should be stored in the refrigerator in a container of water that is changed daily to maintain freshness. Use both fresh tofu and opened shelf-stable tofu within a week.

> **FIRM TOFU,** usually available both refrigerated and shelf-stable, is sold in cakes that weigh between 12 and 18 ounces. Its texture is denser than and holds its shape better than soft and silken tofu. It can be crumbled or cut into cubes, triangles, slabs, or sticks and is good baked or added to stir-fries and stews.
>
> For a firmer, drier texture, press tofu (to remove some of the water) before cooking it. Sandwich the tofu between two plates and weight the top with a heavy object such as a book or can. Press for 15 or 20 minutes.
>
> **FROZEN TOFU:** When you freeze a cake of firm tofu, its texture becomes spongelike. After it is thawed, you can squeeze out quite a bit of water. Then the tofu can be grated or chopped to make a crumbly, chewy addition to soups, stews, and stuffings. It takes at least 6 hours to freeze tofu and about as long to thaw it, so you need to plan ahead. The process can be speeded by slicing the cake of tofu horizontally into two or three slabs before freezing it. Place the tofu on a tray, cover loosely with plastic wrap, and put in the freezer for at least 6 hours. Defrost in the refrigerator or at room temperature, squeeze out the water, and use immediately.
>
> **SOFT TOFU** is sold in cakes like firm tofu. Its texture is between silken and firm, making it ideal for soups, stews, blended sauces, dips, and spreads.
>
> **SILKEN TOFU,** usually sold in boxes, is higher in fat and protein than firm tofu. Its delicate, silky texture and mild flavor make it perfect for desserts, smoothies, and dressings. "Lite" silken tofu has a reduced-fat content.

SEASONED TOFU is a ready-to-eat product stocked in the refrigerator case of most natural foods stores and supermarkets. It is tofu that has been baked or simmered with a variety of spices and flavorings. It is quite firm and can be sliced or grated and used in salads and sandwiches.

TORTILLAS are thin, unleavened flatbreads made from water mixed with wheat flour or corn flour. They commonly range from 4 to 11 inches in diameter. In the United States, packaged corn tortillas are usually on the smaller end of that range and wheat tortillas are on the larger end. Tortillas become pliable when heated and make great wraps for sandwiches, burritos, quesadillas, and enchiladas. In most supermarkets, look in the dairy case or frozen food aisle for brands with no added fat or preservatives.

UDON NOODLES are round, square, or flat Japanese noodles made of wheat flour. Available in natural foods stores, Asian markets, and many supermarkets. Cook udon noodles in a large pot of boiling water until tender, usually 7 to 10 minutes.

VEGETABLE BROTH is our favorite shortcut product for home cooking. At Moosewood Restaurant, we make fresh vegetable stock every day because it gives our soups depth and complexity. But when you're pressed for time, homemade stock just isn't going to happen. So, how can you turn out soups in an instant that still have plenty of flavor like those that simmer half the day? Good news: Quart boxes of organic vegetable, mushroom, and mock chicken broth are on the shelves of most natural foods stores and supermarkets. We like Imagine and Pacific brands.

These broths taste great, have pure ingredients, and can be used directly from the box for soups, stews, and risottos. Once opened, the broth keeps for a few weeks in the refrigerator. Unopened, they sit in your cupboard until you need them. If we were to poll Moosewood cooks, we think these broths would probably be named "favorite convenience product used at home."

ZEST means grated citrus peel, most often lemon, lime, or orange. Zest is made by finely grating the outermost part of the rind. (Don't go deep enough to get into the bitter white pith.) The best tool for zesting is a microplane grater (see page 290).

index

about the authors

The Moosewood Collective is a group of nineteen people who own and operate Moosewood Restaurant. Most of us have worked together for over twenty years, some even longer. Although the word *collective* may evoke an image of indistinguishable worker bees, our collective members are actually quirky, multifaceted individuals. The Moosewood Collective, as the author of cookbooks, is a subset of the larger group, a little different for each book. *Simple Suppers* was written by Laura Branca, Linda Dickinson, Penny Goldin, Susan Harville, David Hirsch, Nancy Lazarus, Wynnie Stein, Jenny Wang, Lisa Wichman, and Kip Wilcox.

Whether we're cooking in the restaurant or on a recipe development team for a cookbook, our work is a blend of fun, stress, social commentary, book and movie reviews, cooking tips, good and bad singing, jokes, remedies for whatever ails you, salty gossip, generosity, and—always—good food. It's theater—luckily, we have a large cast of characters that includes a talented crew of restaurant employees, because the show must go on. Please visit www.moosewoodrestaurant.com for more about us as well as for information on…

conversion chart

American cooks use standard containers, the 8-ounce cup and a tablespoon that takes exactly 16 level fillings to fill that cup level. Measuring by cup makes it very difficult to give weight equivalents, as a cup of densely packed butter will weigh considerably more than a cup of flour. The easiest way therefore to deal with cup measurements in recipes is to take the amount by volume rather than by weight. Thus the equation reads:

1 cup = 240 ml = 8 fl. oz.   ½ cup = 120 ml = 4 fl. oz.

It is possible to buy a set of American cup measures in major stores around the world.

In the States, butter is often measured in sticks. One stick is the equivalent of 8 tablespoons. One tablespoon of butter is therefore the equivalent to ½ ounce/15 grams.

LIQUID MEASURES

FLUID OUNCES	U.S.	IMPERIAL	MILLILITERS
	1 teaspoon	1 teaspoon	5
¼	2 teaspoons	1 dessertspoon	10
½	1 tablespoon	1 tablespoon	14
1	2 tablespoons	2 tablespoons	28
2	¼ cup	4 tablespoons	56
4	½ cup		120
5		¼ pint or 1 gill	140
6	¾ cup		170
8	1 cup		240
9			250, ¼ liter
10	1¼ cups	½ pint	280
12	1½ cups		340
15		¾ pint	420
16	2 cups		450
18	2¼ cups		500, ½ liter
20	2½ cups	1 pint	560
24	3 cups		675
25		1¼ pints	700
27	3½ cups		750
30	3¾ cups	1½ pints	840
32	4 cups or 1 quart		900
35		1¾ pints	980
36	4½ cups		1000, 1 liter
40	5 cups	2 pints or 1 quart	1120

SOLID MEASURES

U.S. and Imperial Measures		Metric Measures	
OUNCES	POUNDS	GRAMS	KILOS
1		28	
2		56	
3½		100	
4	¼	112	
5		140	
6		168	
8	½	225	
9		250	¼
12	¾	340	
16	1	450	
18		500	½
20	1¼	560	
24	1½	675	
27		750	¾
28	1¾	780	
32	2	900	
36	2¼	1000	1
40	2½	1100	
48	3	1350	
54		1500	1½

OVEN TEMPERATURE EQUIVALENTS

FAHRENHEIT	CELSIUS	GAS MARK	DESCRIPTION
225	110	¼	Cool
250	130	½	
275	140	1	Very Slow
300	150	2	
325	170	3	Slow
350	180	4	Moderate
375	190	5	
400	200	6	Moderately Hot
425	220	7	Fairly Hot
450	230	8	Hot
475	240	9	Very Hot
500	250	10	Extremely Hot

Any broiling recipes can be used with the grill of the oven, but beware of high-temperature grills.

EQUIVALENTS FOR INGREDIENTS

all-purpose flour—plain flour
coarse salt—kitchen salt
cornstarch—cornflour
eggplant—aubergine

half and half—12% fat milk
heavy cream—double cream
light cream—single cream
lima beans—broad beans

scallion—spring onion
unbleached flour—strong, white flour
zest—rind
zucchini—courgettes or marrow

AURANTIACEÆ—CITRONS.

...hrubs of evergreen character, having alternate leaves without stipules, with the blade articulated to
...hich is sometimes winged. Flowers fragrant, terminal or axillary, with a short calyx of 3 to 5
...the same in number, white; stamens as many, or some multiple; style simple, stigma enlarged and
...ided. Uncultivated plants have sometimes axillary spines. The leaves are toothed, or entire.
...ipal genus is Citrus, and includes the Orange, Lemon, Lime, Citron, Shaddock and Grape-fruits.
...rs much in shape and size. The Orange is generally globose, the Lemon ovoid, the Citron ovoid and
...haddock spheroidal, and broader at the outer end, and very large. The Grape-fruit is a smaller kind
...but still larger than the Orange, and grows in clusters. The Lime has but small fruit, 1½ inches
...smooth, greenish-yellow rind, and has a pointed tip like the Lemon. All these mentioned are
...xcept Lime and Citron, which are 8 feet. They flower from May to July.
...ts are natives of Asia, particularly of Eastern Asia. The Citron was cultivated in Italy in the
...y the Orange not till the twelfth or fourteenth. The "Golden Apples" of the ancients, and the
...ruit" of the Jews, are supposed to have been some of these.